Making Big Money Investing in Foreclosures

WITHOUT CASH OR CREDIT

Peter Conti & David Finkel

Dearborn™
Trade Publishing
A **Kaplan Professional** Company

Vice President and Publisher: Cynthia A. Zigmund
Acquisitions Editor: Mary B. Good
Senior Managing Editor: Jack Kiburz
Interior Design: Lucy Jenkins
Cover Design: DePinto Studios
Typesetting: Elizabeth Pitts

Published by Dearborn Trade Publishing
A Kaplan Professional Company

Printed in the United States of America

03 04 05 10 9 8 7 6 5 4 3 2

Library of Congress Cataloging-in-Publication Data

Conti, Peter.
   Making big money investing in foreclosures without cash or credit / Peter Conti and David Finkel.
       p. cm.
Includes index.
      ISBN 0-7931-7365-5 (7.25 × 9 paperback)
    1. Real estate investment—United States. 2. Foreclosure—United States. 3. House buying—United States. 4. Real property—United States.   I. Finkel, David.   II. Title.
HD255.C62 2003
332.63′24—dc21

                                                        2003010611

Dedication

To Nino—you succeeded in business with the odds stacked against you. Thanks for showing me what's possible. I know that you will get this message.

Peter Conti

To my best friend, Peter—you have added so much to my life and I love you.

David Finkel

5. THE INSTANT OFFER SYSTEM—FIVE SIMPLE STEPS TO "YES"   135

6. 24 FORECLOSURE PITFALLS THAT CAN COST YOU BIG!   163

7. HOW TO FLIP YOUR DEALS FOR QUICK CASH PROFITS   191

8. INVESTING FOR LONG-TERM WEALTH BUILDUP   211

9. PUTTING IT ALL INTO ACTION   237

As a CPA to the wealthy, I get to really see what they do that's different than the not-so-wealthy. Even more important, because I see the financial statements and tax returns of both groups, I get a picture of what's true beyond all the hype. And the truth is, the wealthy are different! They make their money in different ways, they hold and grow their money differently, and they plan for taxes years in advance. And, there is one consistent truth about the nation's richest people: They all either have made or hold their wealth in real estate.

The secret that the wealthy have learned is that real estate investing has many benefits, including the following:

- *Real estate gives you the ability to make money on other people's money.* You might invest only 10 percent (or much less) in a property, but as the property appreciates in value, your entire investment, including the bank's money, increases.
- *The income you make from real estate is passive.* It's income that your investment makes for you. Instead of you working for your money, your money is working for you.

- *Real estate ownership has tax breaks that are unavailable for any other type of investment.* With real estate, you can take advantage of unique tax advantages, phantom expense (depreciation), low-income housing, ADA improvements and rehabilitation credits, tax-deferred sales of investment property, and the tax-free sale of your principal residence.

Many of my clients are high-income, self-employed taxpayers who have used these real estate loopholes to reduce their taxes while they built wealth. Without real estate as part of the investment and tax plan, they would have to continue to work just to pay their taxes!

If you want to have more money, remember: It's not how much money you make, it's how you make your money that will determine if you get rich.

If Real Estate Is So Great, Why Don't More People Succeed in Real Estate?

Real estate investing requires a different set of skills than other types of investments. For example, you could invest in the stock market via computer and never have to talk to another human being. You could do your research and make all of your trades without ever leaving your home.

That's not the case with real estate. Real estate requires you to interact with people. You need to build a team; negotiate with sellers, buyers, tenants, and lending institutions; handle tenant relationships; and many more items, none of which you were taught in school!

You can learn the skills you need in one of two ways: (1) with a successful mentor who has a proven track record of coaching others, or (2) through the experience of making mistakes and losing money and time. If you have the ability to learn from your mistakes (and recover afterwards), you will likely succeed. However, if you don't have the time or money to make a lot of mistakes, consider having a mentor coach you in building your real estate portfolio and accomplishing your goals.

The other challenge with real estate is that it typically takes more cash to get going than stock investing. You can open an account with a brokerage and start trading on $1,000 or less. On the other hand, real estate properties might run $50,000 (or in some markets $300,000 or more) for the most basic properties. If you don't have or want to spend the cash required for an outright purchase, you're going to need a loan. And typical financing means you need to have good credit and a source of income to repay the loan.

One of the biggest barriers for the first-time buyer is the need for cash and good credit. What if you don't have either? The Mentoring program developed by Peter Conti and David Finkel teaches people how to buy with little or no money of their own, even if they have bad credit. And, I know it works because I've seen the results with their clients.

Why Now Is the Time for Learning to Invest in Foreclosures

Property continues to appreciate at record rates in some markets, and at the same time, foreclosures are at an all-time high. The person facing a foreclosure still needs a place to live, so the overall housing demand doesn't decline, it only changes.

Investing in preforeclosures is a way to enter the real estate market with little money, even with bad or nonexistent credit. You also create win-win solutions by saving other people's credit at the same time you are building your real estate wealth.

Why Using a System Is So Important Now

Real estate investing requires a range of skills that most people haven't been taught. You need to know how to identify deals and opportunities; negotiate with buyers, sellers, renters, and lenders; and then "sell" your properties on a rent-to-own basis for the best possible return. David and Peter have distilled these critical skills into an easy-to-use system.

There is a right way—and a wrong way—to invest in preforeclosures. You are dealing with people whose emotions are high, and you must be careful in structuring deals so they won't unravel later.

There is currently a lot of money chasing a limited amount of real estate, so you need the skills to compete effectively in this market. This book can teach you the tips that Peter and David have learned as they have mentored hundreds of students in these methods.

I'm very honored that David and Peter have asked me to write the Foreword to *Making Big Money Investing in Foreclosures without Cash or Credit,* because I can wholeheartedly endorse their system. They really do what they say, and I've had the opportunity to see many of the deals that they and their students have completed. My husband Richard and I use many of the scripts that they have developed in our own real estate deals. Their ideas work!

–Diane Kennedy, CPA and Tax Strategist

Several very special people are part of our team at Mentor Financial Group, LLC. Over the years, they have helped our students create amazing results and open up new possibilities in their lives. We want to thank them. From our Mentorship selection team of Mike, Tommy, Julia, Byron, Bobby, Theresa, Marie, Jay, and Chuck; to our operations and administration team of Paige, Theresa, Joey, and Pam; to our client-support team of Emily and Sue; to our seminar production leader Bob; to our technology duo of Alex and Mike; to our Mentorship coaches Cheryl, Byron, Scott, and John—you are all OUTSTANDING contributors who really do make a positive difference in the world.

We also want to thank the great team at Dearborn Trade Publishing who not only have done so much to make *Making Big Money Investing in Real Estate without Tenants, Banks, or Rehab Projects* such a huge success, but who put in so much time and effort to make this book such a useful tool to foreclosure investors. A special thank-you to editor Barbara McNichol who spent hours working with us to make this book the best it could be, and to Mary B. Good, acquisitions editor at Dearborn Trade, who helped guide the project along.

This book would never have been written if we didn't receive such loving support and understanding from our wives. Joanna and Heather, thank you for the encouragement and faith you've showered us with.

Our final thank-you goes out to our students. When we sent you an e-mail request to share your stories of foreclosure deals, you literally flooded us with your responses. We are humbled by your generosity. We spent hours around the office reading through all your experiences and were touched by the part you let us play by teaching you through our books, home-study courses, workshops, or Mentorship program. All the stories we share in this book tell of real deals that we and our students completed. While names and descriptions have been changed in some cases, all the relevant details of the stories remain accurate to the best of our knowledge.

You Can Earn up to an Extra $100,000 This Year in Foreclosures

Three years ago, Sarah, a student in our Mentorship program, went from being a highly paid executive of the dot-com boom to an out-of-work statistic of the dot-com bust. Whether you're an executive in the corporate world, a professional person with your own business, or a blue-collar worker with dirt under your nails, you can imagine how scary that reality was for Sarah. Nothing she had learned over the prior 15 years of corporate life had prepared her for the harsh realities of being on her own.

Sarah vowed that never again would she depend on some job or corporation for her income. She decided to start investing in real estate. A few months after she made this decision, Sarah came to one of our workshops in San Diego. She sat right in the front row and took page after page of notes. Hungry to learn how to become successful investing in real estate, she came up and asked questions at every break. How did things turn out for Sarah?

During her first 12 months of investing, she completed ten deals and earned more than $150,000 net profit. Today, she specializes in buying preforeclosures and foreclosure properties in her hometown and earns a lot more money than when she first got started investing.

We're not going to tell you she had it easy—just as many of you won't have it easy—but it can be done. And *you* are the one who can do it.

Over the past eight years, we've been blessed to have helped launch the investing careers of thousands of people across the country. In fact, over that time, our students have bought and sold more than $300 million of real estate. We know we live in a cynical world in which friends and family may say it can't be done. But we're here to tell you that if thousands of our students can do it, you can too.

Mark is a pilot for a large commercial airline who made more than $100,000 from his first foreclosure deal. His greatest dream was to make enough money with his investing that he could quit his airline job and teach high school band classes. Music was his passion and his drive. Mark has now completed many more deals and created a whole new life for himself. If he can have the courage to successfully chase his dreams, you can too.

Cheryl is a stay-at-home mom who started investing without knowing anything about real estate. She was able to buy 14 properties her first 24 months of investing and now buys more than that every year. She specializes in buying foreclosures in her small community. If she could have the faith to step out of her comfort zone and start buying properties, you can too.

Randy is a beginning investor from Hawaii. He finally found his answer for all those people who kept telling him it couldn't be done when he made more than $60,000 on his first foreclosure deal. If Randy can ignore negative influences and realize how big the world of opportunity really is, you can too.

Why the Time Is Now

There has never been a better time to take control of your financial destiny and get out of the rat race. All across the United

States, foreclosure rates are climbing like rockets and bursting onto investors' radar screens. Now is the time to cash in on these unprecedented bargains for yourself and help other people at the same time.

Don't miss out on how big the opportunity is to make money investing in foreclosures. The following indicators have helped drive the foreclosure rate up more than 400 percent over the past 30 years in the United States. And it's only getting higher.

Personal bankruptcy rates are up 400 percent from what they were 40 years ago. Gambling as a percentage of the average person's disposable income has increased by more than 700 percent over the past 40 years. Consumer debt is at an historic high, while savings rates are at historic lows. For the past 30 years, the number of people not covered by health insurance has climbed above 50 percent. (Source: Federal Deposit Insurance Corporation Division of Research and Statistics)

According to the Mortgage Brokers Association of America, 2.3 percent of all residential housing was in various stages of foreclosure by the end of the second quarter of 2002. That's huge! The next time you drive to your local supermarket to shop, you'll probably pass 1,000 homes. Of these, statistically speaking, 23 are in foreclosure. That means in your neighborhood within a few minutes' walk, two or three of your neighbors are going through the process of foreclosing on their homes. These people need your help; as you help them, you'll earn a healthy profit.

Three Biggest Myths about Investing in Foreclosures

All of our lives, well-intentioned people have stated reason after reason why we can't or shouldn't make money investing in foreclosures. But what they told you was only half-true and fully misleading. They passed on their beliefs without even understanding themselves how costly buying into these myths could be for you.

Myth #1: It Takes Money to Make Money

There you are, sitting in your family's dining room after enjoying a full holiday meal. You're a young child; your family is gathered and talking about life. How many times did you see the dreamer in your family get his or her dreams shot down with a bullet like, "You can't do that. Where will you get the money to do it with"?

Were *you* the dreamer in your family who felt the sharp stab from those well-intentioned remarks? Did people who influenced you keep drilling into your head, "It takes money to make money"? Where is this myth written in stone? And if it were really true, how did people like Warren Buffett and Bill Gates start with nothing and build net worths of billions of dollars?

■ Peter's Story

I started investing while I was an auto mechanic working for less than $15 an hour. Not only didn't I have a large chunk of investing capital to start with, but my wife and I had two kids at the time. In the home where I grew up, my dad had to work really hard to provide for his wife and seven kids. One day, I reached an emotional low when my boss yelled at me for helping myself to some coffee that he'd set out for customers. That incident gave me the courage to find a way to make investing work for me. Sometimes it does take an emotional low to help you commit to never settling for less again.   ■

■ David's Story

When I started investing in real estate, I was living in the attic of a converted garage! An injury had just forced me to retire from playing field hockey on the U.S. National team. I was scrimping by on my small savings and finishing up studying for my college degree. That's when I met Peter and he became my real estate mentor. Over the next several years, he helped me buy dozens of properties using other people's money.   ■

It doesn't take money to make money. It takes specialized knowledge of a profitable niche that you apply with disciplined and passionate efforts over time, taking care to learn and improve along the way. Even if it really did take money to make money (which it doesn't), no one said it takes *your own* money to make money. One of the advantages of investing in foreclosures is that it's easy to use other people's money to make money. You can potentially tap into thousands of dollars in profits created through buying properties using other sources of funding.

Myth #2: You Need Good Credit to Borrow Money

We can hear you saying, "Yeah, but we need good credit to borrow money so we can make money investing in foreclosures."

This is true if your only source of funding is from traditional lenders. In this book, you'll learn seven other ways to fund your way into a deal with someone else's money—no matter what your credit is like.

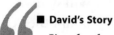

■ **David's Story**

I've had a hand in hundreds of real estate deals—acquiring interest in millions of dollars worth of real estate—yet I've only applied for funds through a conventional lender for *two* loans in all those years. If I can do this, you can too. It's just a matter of learning the real-world secrets that successful investors have mastered.

For example, I bought and made more than $100,000 in profits from a five-bedroom, three-and-a-half-bath house. The seller agreed to act as my bank and carry back all the financing I needed to buy that property after a small down payment. He carried back over $400,000 without ever once asking to check my credit. Was the seller unsophisticated? Was I taking advantage of him? No. He had a net worth several times greater than mine (he was a real estate investor in his 70s and I was just 28 years old at the time). He regarded this as a win-win situation.   ■

When you understand and apply the ideas in this book, you'll learn that motivated sellers don't care about your credit; they don't care about your home life; they don't care about *you,* period. *They care about getting out of tough situations and relieving themselves of major sources of pain in their lives.* And sellers are only one of several funding sources for your foreclosure deals.

Myth #3: If You Buy a Property from a Seller in Foreclosure, You're a Shark Taking Advantage of Another Person's Misery

This false belief would have you believe that you are out there swindling sellers by sneaking into their home, fooling them into signing documents, and running away with all their cash before they wake up to what you're doing. Far from it!

Even if some investors do business that way, let's make it absolutely clear that's *not* how we're teaching you to do business. When you help sellers in foreclosure, they are thankful for your taking time to understand their situations and finding a win-win way to solve a problem they're embarrassed and scared to admit they even have.

Investing in foreclosures is like holding the core of your being up to a mirror. If you are a good person, what reflects back is that you help people and get paid well for doing it. Isn't that what business is all about—providing value and getting paid handsomely for that?

The Choice Is Yours

When we tell people, "Anyone can make big money investing in foreclosures," most simply shake their heads and walk away. We watch them passing on what might be their best chance to create security and freedom for themselves and their families. They simply don't believe—or can't believe—they could be successful this way. They say they don't have enough money, or that they don't know how, or that it's too hard. Sadly, many let themselves sink into "lives of quiet desperation" that so many people lead.

But you're different. Something inside made you realize it's possible *for you* to create your fortune with real estate. You may not have all the know-how yet, but with the specialized knowledge you'll gain from reading this book, you'll uncover dozens of ways to find profitable foreclosure deals and structure them without using your cash or credit.

We know this sounds too good to be true. But success takes a great deal of study, disciplined action, and willingness to set aside many deeply rooted beliefs you have about wealth. If you are willing to add these three ingredients to the recipes explained in this book, we guarantee you *can* and *will* make big money investing in foreclosures.

2

The Big Picture of Investing in Foreclosures

Investing in foreclosures and preforeclosures is a rewarding and profitable niche for investors. Anyone with the right attitude, the specialized knowledge, and the willingness to practice and learn along the way can make money investing in foreclosures.

This chapter defines foreclosure, explains the concepts involved when buying foreclosures, and walks you through several sample deals. It includes examples of how other investors have made healthy profits structuring deals with sellers of foreclosure and preforeclosure properties.

As you read through these stories, do your best to get a feel for how these deals flow and the common elements among them. Chapter 3 explains how to structure each type of these deals. For the moment, though, it's important to understand that you *can* make money buying foreclosures without cash or credit.

Foreclosure Defined

Foreclosure is the legal process by which a person or institution that is owed money can force the sale of a property to pay off the money that a borrower owes. Before getting deeper into the process, let's introduce some of the key players in the foreclosure game.

Bankers

When people go to a bank to borrow money, they're asked to sign two important documents: a *promissory note* and a security instrument (either a *deed of trust* or a *mortgage.*)

The promissory note is the IOU or acknowledgment of debt. It says the borrower owes the bank a specific amount of money and lists the exact terms of the loan and the required repayment.

Imagine you were an officer at the bank. Would you give applicants $300,000 based on their word alone? Wouldn't you want a guarantee that you would indeed get your money back? This guarantee is the security instrument that, depending on what state you're investing in, will be either a deed of trust or a mortgage.

However, the deed of trust or mortgage is *not* an IOU or a promissory note; it is a security agreement. It states that the borrower will repay the loan and live up to the terms and conditions of the loan, or the lender can force the sale of the property to raise the money to pay for as much of the outstanding loan as possible.

Think about it this way: The loan process is like a teenager asking his parents for permission to borrow the car Saturday night. The teenager gives his best pleading performance to borrow the car, saying, "Please, Mom and Dad. I want to take Sally out to the movies. I've always been responsible when you let me borrow the car in the past . . ." Just as the teenager tries to convince his parents to lend him the car, so do loan applicants present the best possible case of their ability to repay the loan. They even show proof of their good credit history (like the teenager declaring to his parents, "I've always been responsible in the past").

Finally, the parents give in and grant permission for the teenager to borrow the car *but* they lay down certain ground rules the teenager must follow: He must be home by 11 PM; he must tell them exactly where he is going, with whom, and when. Setting out the rules for lending the car is what a banker does in a promissory note—including specific terms and conditions of the loan and how and when it will be repaid.

But smart parents, just like smart bankers, know they also need to establish the consequences of what will happen if the teenager doesn't live up to his side of the agreement. "If you're not home by 11 PM or if you change your plans without getting our approval first, or if you are reckless with the car, then you will be grounded and lose all car privileges for a period of time." Bankers establish consequences too, although they take it about ten steps further. They make the borrower sign a deed of trust or mortgage that establishes the negative consequences if the borrower doesn't live up to all the terms and conditions of the promissory note.

The language in the deed of trust or mortgage says, for example, the borrower agrees to keep the property properly insured, agrees to properly maintain the property, and, of course, agrees to make timely payments on the promissory note. If the borrower doesn't live up to these terms, then bankers apply the consequences stated in the deed of trust or mortgage—specifically, they foreclose on the house.

What Foreclosure Deals Look Like

Deal One

One of our Mentorship students found a couple about to lose their home to foreclosure. After several conversations with this couple, we agreed to buy their house worth $175,000 for what was owed on it, plus the back payments. (The loan had an outstanding balance of $155,000 and back payments totaled $9,000.) We also agreed to give the seller $1,000 cash. We simply took over making the payments to the lender on the loan the sellers already had in place. Four years later, we still own this property. To date, we've made more than $125,000 at appreciation from this property plus we receive a cash flow of $250 a month from renting it out.

Deal Two

Michael, one of our students in New Orleans, found a motivated seller with a junker of a house. He put the property under contract to buy for $20,000. Its "after repair value" was $60,000 and it needed about $15,000 in repairs. Not wanting to get involved with a rehab project (not to mention that he didn't have the $35,000 cash needed to buy and fix up the property himself), Michael sold his contract to another investor for $2,200 cash—his first of six deals during his first six months of investing.

Deal Three

Another student, Sally, bought a VA (Department of Veterans Affairs) foreclosure house and rehabbed the property. To fund the deal, Sally borrowed the money from her mother and agreed to pay it back at 9 percent interest when she resold the property. Sally kept the house as a rental for a while, paying her mom "interest only" payments every month and enjoying a positive cash flow since she bought the house so inexpensively. Last year, Sally resold the property and netted $35,000! In fact, Sally was so excited about this first deal, she started a second one right away. She borrowed the needed $5,000 down payment from her credit union to pay to a seller in preforeclosure, then took over the payments on the seller's loan. As a result, she got $15,000 of equity and a positive cash flow from day one. She currently has more than $52,000 of equity in this one deal alone.

Deal Four

Gina, a full-time investor who read our book *Making Big Money Investing in Real Estate,* found a motivated seller who had moved from Colorado Springs, Colorado, to California because of a job change. The seller was about to lose his Colorado property to foreclosure when Gina helped him find a way out. The house was valued at $400,000 with two liens against it: a first mortgage of $351,000 and a second mortgage of $25,000. The seller wanted to save his credit from being ruined by a foreclosure; he knew he wouldn't get any money out of the sale. So Gina negotiated with the first mortgage holder to accept a *short sale* (discussed in Chapter 3) in the amount of $300,000 and the second mortgage holder to accept $8,000 as full payment for the money owed. This meant Gina was able to buy that $400,000 house for a total price of $308,000. Then she resold the house 30 days later for $360,000. After all closing costs, she netted $30,000. It was a win-win-win deal for everyone. The seller was thrilled to save his credit; the buyer was thrilled to save $40,000 on the purchase of his home; Gina was thrilled to make a healthy profit of $30,000.

Deal Five

Maggie, a Mentorship student from North Carolina, found a motivated seller who was about to lose a house she'd inherited from her mother because of foreclosure. Instead of fixing up the house and keeping it, Maggie sold her contract to another investor for $15,000 and gave $5,000 of that money to the seller. Pleased with the outcome, the seller sent Maggie a note that read: *"Thank you so very much. You've been a blessing to me. Before my mother died, she asked me not to lose her property. So this has been very painful for me. Thank you for helping me."*

Homeowners in foreclosure are going through a lot because they're dealing with the personal anguish of a very public failure.

Add to this their possible feelings of shame, failure, and embarrassment and you've got the picture. They may also feel depressed and on the defensive. Some may simply be in denial, waiting for a knight in shining armor (or lottery winnings) to save the day. Many behave indecisively because they're confused about what's happening to them. So when you help sellers get out of tough places, you help them move on. You are providing a great service.

What You Can Offer a Homeowner Facing Foreclosure

As a knowledgeable investor, you can benefit many of these homeowners by:

- Helping them save their credit
- Helping them salvage some or all of their equity
- Helping them end an embarrassing situation
- Helping them release some of the worry and stress they feel
- Giving them a fast solution to their foreclosure problem
- Providing expert help in deciding what to do next, maybe even handling all of the details

Deficiency Judgments

Many homeowners think that once the foreclosure sale is over, their worries end. This may not be true. In many states, the lender can get a *deficiency judgment* from the court. This means the borrower (homeowner) still owes the lender any money that the lender *lost* from the whole process. Many times this pushes the homeowner to declare bankruptcy to escape this debt burden.

Because the law doesn't allow the lender to make a profit on a foreclosure, any money made at the foreclosure sale in excess of the amount owed the lender, including the foreclosure costs, will go to the borrower. However, rarely does the borrower get anything for his or her equity in a foreclosure sale because the house is usually sold well below market price.

The lender can receive money for such fees as:

- Late penalties
- Accrued interest
- Attorney's fees
- Court costs
- Filing fees
- Title work fees

Deed of Trust versus Mortgage

Each state has specific laws about how the foreclosure process operates in that state. One big distinction is whether your state uses a *deed of trust* to secure real estate loans or a *mortgage.*

While some states use both, all states use one or the other of these documents in the majority of loans. So find out if your state is a deed of trust state or a mortgage state by asking a local title company or real estate attorney which document is commonly used. You can also log on to Your Bonus Web Pack, which includes a chart showing which type of state you are investing in. (For more information, see "Your Bonus Web Pack" at the back of the book.)

A deed of trust and a mortgage perform essentially the same role, namely, securing the lender's loan to a borrower. Let's explain some important differences.

A deed of trust is a three-party agreement involving these players:

1. *Trustor:* The borrower
2. *Trustee:* A third party the bank chooses to look after the bank's interests
3. *Beneficiary:* The lender.

When people borrow money in a deed of trust state, they sign a document (deed of trust) that gives legal title to the property to a trustee for the benefit of the lender (beneficiary). Now, the borrower really owns the property and has all kinds of rights to enjoy the property *up to a point.* The borrower cannot do anything that will jeopardize the lender's security in the house (like let it go into disrepair). Also, the borrower cannot stop paying the lender its money without the trustee foreclosing on the house.

In a deed of trust state, the process of foreclosure is also called a *nonjudicial foreclosure* because the foreclosure process doesn't take place in a courtroom in front of a judge; it happens by a *trustee's sale* of the property. The trustee must follow a specific set of rules established in each state. The final step is the sale of the property by an auction run by the trustee for the benefit of the lender (beneficiary).

A mortgage, while used for essentially the same purpose, has some important differences. First, a mortgage is only a two-party agreement between the mortgagor (borrower) and mortgagee (lender).

With a mortgage, there is no third-party trustee to look after the lender's interest; the lender does this itself. When a mortgagor (the person who borrowed the money) defaults on the terms and conditions of the mortgage (the most important of which is to make timely payments to the lender as spelled out in the promissory note), the lender (mortgagee) proceeds with a *judicial foreclosure* on the property. It's called a judicial foreclosure because it takes place in a courtroom before a judge. Typically, a judicial foreclosure used in mortgage states takes longer than a trustee's sale.

Remember, each state has its own way of doing things and you will need to research and learn the legal ropes in your area.

Nonjudicial Foreclosures (Trustee's Sales)

Here's how the foreclosure process for a nonjudicial or trustee's sale foreclosure works. It applies in states that use deeds of trust.

Step One: Borrower Is Delinquent— Preforeclosure Stage

The borrower misses a payment on his or her loan and, after the grace period, he falls delinquent on the loan.

Because foreclosures are costly to lenders and they prefer to collect payments and not take back houses, most lenders will work with a homeowner for a period of time, typically 60 to 90 days, before they go to Step Two of the foreclosure process.

Step Two: Lender Files the Default—Notice of Default Stage

At a certain point, the lender will no longer work with the borrower and will start the official legal process of foreclosing on the property. The lender files a Notice of Default (NOD) at the county recorder's office and mails a certified copy of the NOD to the borrower. In some states the name of this document is different, but its purpose and function is always the same. In Colorado, for example, the document that lenders use to record the default is called Notice of Election and Demand for Sale by Public Trustee. That's just a long way of saying an official notice that the foreclosure clock is ticking. (Note: In Your Bonus Web Pack, we've included a state-by-state listing of the exact process used by lenders to foreclose on the property and the document used to start the foreclosure clock ticking.)

During this stage, the borrower may reinstate the loan. This means the borrower can make up the back payments and late fees, bringing the loan back into good standing. If the borrower does re-instate the loan, then the foreclosure stops. If the borrower doesn't, the foreclosure process moves on to the next step.

Step Three: Lender Prepares to Force Sale of Property—Notice of Sale Stage

If the borrower doesn't bring the loan current during the 60 to 90 days following the Notice of Default, the lender will move ahead with plans to force the sale of the property. This sale is called a trustee's sale because the trustee of the deed of trust that the bor-rower signed conducts the auction.

In stage three of the foreclosure process, the lender records a Notice of Sale and advertises the pending foreclosure sale in a general-circulation newspaper for three to six weeks. In some states, once the Notice of Sale (or the comparable document) is recorded, the borrower no longer can reinstate the loan, but instead must pay off the outstanding balance. In other states, such as California, the borrower has up to five business days before the sale date to reinstate the loan. (Check "Your Bonus Web Pack" at the back of the book for more details.)

Step Four: Trustee Conducts the Trustee's Sale— Public Auction

We finally reach the courthouse steps. The trustee auctions the property off to the highest bidder who must pay in cash or cer-tified funds. At this auction, the lender opens bidding with the amount of money owed (including late fees and other foreclosure costs) and if no one bids higher than that amount, the bank keeps the property. If someone does bid higher, that person has a set amount of time (usually a few hours or sometimes immediately) to produce the certified funds to purchase the property. Then the trustee executes a Trustee's Deed to the new owner.

Step Five: Buyer Waits for Redemption Period to Pass—Redemption Period

The redemption period is a period of time after the foreclosure auction during which the borrower can get the full amount of what was owed (including all fees and other foreclosure costs) to the trustee and get the property back. Meanwhile, the investor (or lender) who "purchased" the property at the auction has to wait out the redemption period. If the homeowner redeems the loan, the trustee refunds money paid to the lender/investor and returns the title to the property to the homeowner.

During this period, the homeowner usually lives in the house for free while determining where to move next. The lender or investor who "got" the house at auction cannot harass or remove the homeowner until the redemption period has expired. (Note: In the rare case of the lender or investor showing a court that the homeowner is damaging the house and radically diminishing its value, that person may be able to get court permission to remove the homeowner.)

In most deed of trust states, the homeowner has *no* redemption rights but it varies. In some states, such as Colorado, the homeowner does have a redemption period of 75 days. Almost all mortgage states have redemption periods.

Judicial Foreclosures (Used in Mortgage States)

Step One: Borrower Is Delinquent—Preforeclosure Stage

The borrower misses a payment on his loan and after the grace period is ended becomes delinquent on the loan. This step is the same in both a judicial and a nonjudicial foreclosure. The lender prefers not to foreclose but to have the borrower make timely payments.

Once the lender believes it's at risk of not getting the money, it quickly proceeds to Step Two—which *does* differ from the nonjudicial process.

Step Two: Lender Files a Lawsuit—Judicial Foreclosure Begins

The lender files an official document with the courts (a Complaint) that initiates the lawsuit to foreclose on the property. The lender also needs to give outside parties notice that the lawsuit is occurring by recording a *lis pendens* with the county recorder. This tells the world there's a "lawsuit pending" on the property; anyone who has an interest in the property can take the appropriate steps to protect his or her interests. The borrower may answer the complaint, which keeps the lender from getting a default judgment and slows down the process.

> *Insider Secret:* One of the biggest challenges you face when investing in foreclosures is the increasing time pressure you must work under. One insider secret is to help the borrower file an answer to a lender's complaint. This sounds more complicated than it is. In reality, filing an answer is quick and easy and will delay the foreclosure process by up to a month. So just by helping your seller file this document, you gain up to 30 days of time to figure out how you'll purchase the property!

Step Three: Lender and Borrower Meet in Court

If the borrower has filed an answer with the court to the lender's complaint, then a court date is scheduled, when the judge will decide if the lender has the right to proceed with the foreclosure (which is the normal outcome of this hearing). If the court rules in the favor of the lender, it issues a judgment and sets a sale date.

Step Four: The Sheriff's Sale

Typically three to four weeks after the sheriff's sale is advertised, the auction takes place and the property is sold to the highest bidder. Once the sheriff's sale happens, a Certificate of Sale is issued to the buyer. In most states the previous owner has the right to redeem (buy back) the property for a set period of time, often 12 months. A sheriff's sale is functionally the same thing as a trustee's sale.

Step Five: Buying the House Back after the Sale— Redemption Period

The main difference in the redemption period in a judicial foreclosure in mortgage states is that almost all mortgage states *have* a redemption period. Also, the redemption period is typically longer in mortgage states than in deed of trust states—up to 12 months in some states. If the borrower doesn't redeem the property during this time, the new buyer gets title to the property through a fancy document called a Sheriff's Deed.

> *Insider Secret:* In many states, the homeowner can *sell* his redemption rights to a third party—an investor like you! Imagine a case in which a house is auctioned and no one outbids the lender, but you *know* the house is worth significantly more. You connect with the owner and pay that person to assign his redemption rights to you. Then you use the redemption period to raise funds to pay the money owed to the lender (including all costs, penalties,

and accrued interest) and buy the house back. Sometimes the best deals can be made after the game appears to be over.

What happens to the homeowner after the foreclosure auction? It depends. If the borrower has any redemption rights (usually the case if the lender used a judicial foreclosure), then the new owner of the property must typically wait until the entire redemption period is over before getting the homeowner out of the property. If the property is rented, the new owner will require that the tenants pay the rent to him. After the borrower's redemption rights have expired or immediately after a trustee's sale (for nonjudicial foreclosure), the new owner files an eviction action—usually called an *unlawful detainer*—against the occupant. Unless the trustee made a serious mistake in the foreclosure process, the judge almost always sides with the new owner.

Best Foreclosure Stage to Buy In

Which stage is best to buy in? While there are advantages to buying in each stage, our preference is to buy in the first one—pre-foreclosure—for three reasons:

1. *You have much less competition.* Because you've found most of these deals before other investors even know about them, you'll be able to negotiate one-to-one with the seller without other investors knocking at the door. This gives you the chance to negotiate a better deal. Remember, once a foreclosure officially starts, every investor in town knows about it and will be mailing, calling, or visiting the home-owner.
2. *You can get into investing with very little money.* When the foreclosure process is in the early stages, the home-owner tends to owe less money in back payments. Combine

this fact with a simple yet powerful technique called *subject to financing* (see Chapter 3) and sellers may be willing to deed you the property in exchange for your making up the back payments and taking over the burden of the monthly payments. The seller gets a fast out and saves his credit, and you buy another investment property that often has a positive cash flow from day one (plus a chunk of equity). You also get to leverage your way into the deal without taking on the liability of personally guaranteeing any debt.

3. *You have plenty of time to find a solution.* Because the foreclosure hasn't technically started, you have at least a few months to close on the property and find your end user for the property (whether it's another investor to sell the deal to or a tenant buyer to sell the house to on a rent-to-own basis or any of a number of different exit strategies).

Your second-best choice is to buy during the reinstatement period. In many states, even after the foreclosure has technically started, you can still make up the back payments and reinstate the loan. You bring the loan up-to-date and make payments every month as the seller did before getting behind. The major benefit to buying this way is that you can still use the existing financing as a way to leverage yourself into the deal. The downside is that once the official foreclosure has started, you'll encounter a lot more competition from other investors who now know about the seller's situation.

Your third-best choice is buying after the sale has occurred, either from the bank or by buying the seller's redemption rights.

If you plan on being a cash buyer (and carefully read Chapter 3 before you decide you *can't* be a cash buyer), then buying directly from a bank might work well for you. Once a foreclosure auction takes place in which no one bids more than the bank's bid, the property goes back to the bank and becomes a Real Estate Owned (REO) property. It gets sold as quickly as possible by the lender who isn't in the housing business but the lending business. Therefore, you can often get hefty discounts on these properties.

Also, once a property has been sold at auction, the seller still has the right to redeem the loan and buy back the property in many states. As an investor, one strategy is to find a seller who's willing to sell you his redemption rights, then you buy back the property. This can be a highly profitable way to buy.

Ultimately, the biggest benefit of buying after the auction is that most investors think the game is over so you tend to have less competition. Also, you aren't under a time crunch anymore. This means you can actually take the time to properly conduct your due diligence and have the property professionally inspected.

Your fourth-best choice is buying during the final days up to the actual sale date. While you can still make many profitable deals happen at this late stage, it's stressful and hurried, plus it requires access to a lot of cash in most cases.

■ David's Story

I remember one house we bought in an area of San Diego called Chula Vista. The house was a three-bedroom, two-bath home in a nice area. The sellers were at the final stages of a foreclosure that they had dragged out as long as they could by declaring bankruptcy. We felt pressure to close fast, both from the sellers and from the lender. All along, we let the sellers know they would net about $25,000 after their share of all the closing costs. The sellers were happy with that; they left me three voice-mail messages in a week saying how grateful they were, and how they understood that they would be getting around $25,000.

Well, the closing date came and after all the costs were added up, the sellers ended up with a net check for $24,500. This was almost exactly the amount of money I had told them to expect. The next week, I got two messages from the sellers yelling at me at how unhappy they were with the money they received and how it was all so unfair to them.

This was the first time I'd ever seen such an about-face in sellers. Since that time, I've seen it on other occasions when the seller was in the final stages of foreclosure. I've come to realize that it isn't about sellers being bad people; they're simply in an extremely stressful and scary place. Some people faced with these pressures don't react well and look for other people to lash out at. If you are going to buy during this stage of the foreclosure, be aware of this possibility and keep yourself emotionally whole. This took me quite a while to learn. ∎

Our last choice is buying at the actual auction itself. While many experienced investors make a great living buying properties at the actual foreclosure auctions, we tend to avoid buying at this stage for three reasons:

1. It takes all cash to play this game! This means no leverage unless you have a private investor backing you up.
2. We believe it's the riskiest stage you can buy in because you won't be able to inspect the houses or take your time to conduct your due diligence. When you combine this lack of due diligence with the need for an all-cash closing, you're taking a big risk unless you really know what you're doing.
3. The auction process itself generally favors the selling party. We've dealt with enough houses to know that you never want to be in a group of other buyers competing for the same house. This competition—combined with the natural human fear of losing a great deal—are two potent psychological factors working against you.

Here's one exception to buying at auction: If you are the only bidder and you have checked out the house (and if you're experienced), then go ahead and bid on it. How can you be the only investor at the auction? Check out several auctions and get to know the other regulars. Ask them which times and days tend to have the fewest competitors. Just in case they aren't willing to share that information, look for a property where the auction date was postponed. Other investors may miss the delayed auction so you might be the only one showing up to bid.

Study the Rules

Our advice is to buy as early in the foreclosure process as possible because that's when you're likely to make the most money. We and our students have profited in the tens of millions of dollars by buying distressed houses directly from the owners before the house is sold at auction. We believe this is the easiest entry point to immediately start making money investing in foreclosures.

As an investor, you'll have to become familiar with the "rules" and legal process of foreclosure in your state. (You can get a good start by checking out your state's laws in "Your Bonus Web Pack" at the end of the book.) Know what things can stall a foreclosure process to give you, the investor, more time. For example, just by filing an answer to the lender's complaint in some states can buy you an extra *month* of time. Or, for example, in California, if the lender puts down the wrong information on the Notice of Default, you can force the lender to start all over with the paperwork, which can buy you as much as two to three months of time.

Remember, it's just a game. To get good at playing it, you've got to study the rules. Just like champion athletes have to put the effort in on the practice field, wealthy investors have to invest the time and energy to master the rules of the game. It's not glamorous, but it's the truth.

In the next chapter, you'll learn 12 specific strategies to structure moneymaking deals without your cash or credit.

3

12 Ways to Structure Deals without Cash or Credit

How should you structure your offers to put together deals? You are about to learn the 12 best foreclosure buying strategies. Whether you are buying properties in foreclosure or in preforeclosure, these strategies will allow you to start making money investing in foreclosures right away.

If you read our book *Making Big Money Investing in Real Estate*, you'll be familiar with a few of these buying strategies. But you'll notice that we have completely left out any discussion of buying with a *lease option*. A lease option is when you lease out a property from a seller for a long period of time with an agreed-on option price at which you can buy the property at any point during the lease period. When buying foreclosures, a lease option is *not* the way you'll want to structure the deal. (It's still a great way to buy homes in nice areas with nothing down; it's just not the best strategy to use with foreclosure deals.) Rather, we want to share 12 other cutting-edge strategies that have four factors in common.

Four Factors That Make Purchase Option Strategies Work with Foreclosures

1. Little or No Money Down

You can make all these buying strategies work without putting a ton of your cash into the property deals. For the buying strategies that do require cash, you'll learn how to minimize the amount of your money in the deal by tapping into insider sources to fund your deals.

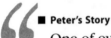

■ Peter's Story

One of our students found an REO (Real Estate Owned) property that a lender had taken back in a foreclosure. Using VA financing, our student was able to buy this $170,000 five-bedroom house for just $117,100 (including $6,800 of closing costs). After talking with her local bank manager, this student was able to get all the closing costs rolled into the loan, so that she put nothing down. She then went out and sold the house for $159,000 in a quick sale. Not bad for a "zero-down" deal.   ■

2. Find Funding, Even If Your Credit Is Bad

You can use all these buying strategies regardless of the condition of your credit. Some nontraditional funding sources for your deals could care less if your credit has holes in it the size of Texas. You'll learn how to tap into these specialized sources of financing that serious investors have been using for decades to make themselves millions of dollars. (The ideas you'll learn have been called the "best-kept secrets of millionaire investors.")

■ David's Story

Over the past seven years, I've had my hand in more than a hundred deals and, with the exception of only two properties, my credit has never been an issue. By that I mean the seller or person I got the money from never ran a credit check. I know this sounds impossible, but when you use the ideas in this book, you'll realize that while good credit can help, it's *not* a requirement for making money investing in foreclosures.   ■

3. Minimize Your Risk

Making money is important, but keeping the money you make is equally important. All these purchase option foreclosure strategies help you isolate and minimize your risk.

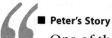

■ Peter's Story

One of the properties I bought years ago when I started investing was a two-bedroom condo that I purchased with conventional bank financing with a healthy chunk of my own money as a down payment and a personal guarantee on the loan. One time, a tenant who had some unsavory friends was living in my unit. The police came and knocked on my tenant's door to talk with these "friends" who broke the back window and jumped out the second story window to run for it. Looking back, I still remember how much emotional stress that tenant caused me.

Fast-forward to a deal I did using the Purchase Option ideas you are learning. I have an investment property in Colorado Springs that was vacant for two months. Because I had none of my money into the deal and no personal guarantee on the financing, I didn't feel anywhere close to the same amount of stress as I felt in the past. I simply fired the property management company and got someone else to take over and fill the vacancy. It felt like a Monopoly game—as if I were losing a little money in a game rather than the highly personal feeling of having my hard-earned cash at risk on the condo. That's the way I like to do my investing now—to potentially risk some of my profit, but to never have my capital or credit at stake.   ■

4. Help Sellers Win

You will be working with sellers who need your help. When you buy a foreclosure property the right way, you create a win-win transaction that helps sellers effectively deal with tough personal situations.

■ **David's Story**
I purchased a three-bedroom house in San Diego on which the sellers had gotten five payments behind on their mortgage. The husband was fairly ill and I remember going back over to the house after we had signed the contract and talking with his wife. After a few minutes, she asked me to walk with her into the bedroom because her husband wanted to see me. As we walked in and I saw the husband stretched out in the bed, I felt awkward. But then he started to thank me for helping them make the best of a bad situation. He was having serious back problems and couldn't work. They were about to lose the house when I offered to help them with a better way out. I left that day knowing I'd made a difference as an investor.   ■

Traditional Ways to Buy Foreclosures

Before explaining our Purchase Option buying strategies, let's describe how most people invest in foreclosures so you can see the benefits of using the Purchase Option foreclosure strategies described in this book.

Traditionally, most investors buying foreclosures sought houses they could get good prices on (either directly with the owner, through a real estate agent, at an auction, or directly from the bank) for an *all-cash closing*. This meant either the investors took the money out of their personal bank accounts or borrowed from a traditional lender. Truth be told, this was a good way to invest and these investors made lots of money. But the majority of people who wanted to get started investing found themselves excluded because they didn't have the cash or credit to do these deals the traditional way.

Also, while these traditional investors made money, in many cases they took on magnitudes of risk—risk they easily could have avoided by using the strategies you are about to learn.

Let's be clear, any way you structure a deal that allows you to purchase a foreclosure and make a profit in a win-win way is fine by us. Even if you just want to use our ideas to fine-tune your traditional foreclosure investing, this book gives you the tools and techniques to do this. If you're looking for more than that—if you want buying strategies that are simple yet powerful enough that they work regardless of the quality of your credit or the size of your bank account—you'll find these powerful ideas will supercharge your investing profits.

■ David's Story

It surprises many beginning investors when I recommend that, even if they do have money or great credit, they get started investing *without* using their own cash or conventional bank loans. They find it hard to believe that sometimes having money can be detrimental to learning to be the best investor you can be. I've seen money used as a crutch to make a marginal deal go through. I admit I've been guilty of getting lazy and throwing money into a deal where a little more imagination and prudent negotiation would have served me better. But with an open mind and the right education, not having money can be a force to push you to be a faster, more creative, and more skilled investor.

What's more, you'd be surprised how fast you can pour your liquid cash reserves into real estate. I've watched traditional investors pour more than $1,000,000 into several deals in a matter of months and then have to wait until they sold those properties before they could free up enough of their money to go out and buy more properties. You'll never regret learning to buy without money. It will make you a much more savvy investor for those times you *do* decide to use your own money or conventional financing.   ■

The Foundational Foreclosure Buying Strategy

If you are just getting started investing, structuring deals with sellers in foreclosure can seem overwhelming as you try to remember the various ways of conducting them. If you were locked into using only one buying strategy with sellers in foreclosure, however, the one we recommend is buying properties subject to the seller's loan. It's that powerful.

If you read *Making Big Money Investing in Real Estate,* you already know we often use a lease option as the foundational technique when buying investment properties from motivated sellers who *aren't* in foreclosure. This buying strategy is the foundational buying strategy for working with homeowners who *are* in foreclosure.

When beginning Mentorship students come through our workshops, they struggle with information overload. It can be compared to a new mechanic who is given a toolbox with an overwhelming number of unfamiliar and specialized tools. That's why we highly encourage you to master one or two tools first. Once you get comfortable using those tools, then layer in another tool, then another and another.

As you read through this chapter with all its buying strategies, you don't need to "get" them all on the first go-around. Lock onto one or two buying strategies that you can put to work making you

---

FIGURE 3.1   Assessing the Costs

After-repair value of house	$225,000
Current "as is" value of house	$200,000
Needed repairs (paint, carpet, etc.)	$ 4,000
Existing first mortgage	$190,000
PITI payments on first mortgage	$ 1,350
Back payments owed	$ 4,000

---

money, then add in other layers of strategies later. If you have too many options at once, you run the risk of freezing up when meeting with a seller.

Imagine you were meeting with a motivated seller in the early stages of foreclosure and that seller owns a well-kept house in an area you like. You sit down with this owner and after you've spent time getting to know her situation thoroughly, she says, "I just want out. I don't care about the equity. I just want to walk away from the house. I'm at the end of my rope and if you don't want to buy it for what I owe, then I'll just let the bank come and take it."

You see the seller looking right at you and know all she wants is to stop this foreclosure that's draining all her energy. The house is worth $200,000. With $4,000 worth of paint and carpeting, it would probably be worth $225,000. She owes $190,000 as a first mortgage with monthly payments of principal, interest, real estate taxes, and insurance (PITI) totaling $1,350 (see Figure 3.1).

She's got two real problems. First, she's behind three months in her payments. With late fees, that comes to more than $4,000—money she simply doesn't have. Second, even if she could find a way to make up the back payments, she still has no way of scraping together $1,350 each month after that. More than anything, she just wants you to take the house for what she owes and she'll go find a place to rent for $800 a month, which is all she can really afford.

Many investors would look at this situation and calculate if it makes sense to take $200,000 cash to buy a house worth $225,000.

(The $200,000 cash is the total cost for the property of paying off the $190,000 loan, plus the $4,050 of back payments, plus $4,000 of cosmetic work, plus $2,000 of closing costs.) But if you were a cash buyer, this deal wouldn't work for you because that $25,000 of equity would get eaten up quickly with holding costs, plus the closing costs of the second closing once you resold the house.

Some investors might go ahead and buy it anyway with the intention of holding the house as a long-term rental. Fair enough, but it really wasn't much of a bargain for a cash purchase.

Other investors would try to get that $200,000 (or a large chunk of it) by borrowing it from a conventional lender. While this would be a way to leverage your way into the deal, it comes with three main disadvantages.

1. The cost of the money. After adding up all the costs of getting that new loan, you would have eaten up around $5,000 of your equity. Here are some of those costs that make your banker, not you, rich:

- Loan origination fee
- Prepaid interest or "points"
- Credit check fee
- Property appraisal
- Document delivery fees
- Recording fees

2. Your lender will require that you sign personally on the loan. That means if anything goes wrong with the house or the housing market in your area, regardless of whose fault it is, your credit (and potentially other assets) are on the line.

3. You'll have to jump through the hoops of qualifying for traditional financing. That requires credit checks, long loan applications, bank statements, and tax returns the lender wants to review. And just when you thought it had everything, your lender almost always finds two or three more things. Does it tell you about all this up front? No! The lender waits until the week before you're supposed to close. So you spend the last week before closing scrambling to make the deal work. (Notice that we're just a bit jaded about this.)

Who needs all that stress? Wouldn't it be better to step in and take over making payments on the seller's loan? You can do this once you have the specialized knowledge you are about to learn.

The Best-Kept Secret in Real Estate— Buying "Subject To"

Over the years, thousands of investors across the country have asked us to mentor them to become financially free. If you were one of our Mentorship students and brought this deal to us to discuss, here's how we'd coach you through the deal:

You: The seller just wants to walk away from the house and doesn't want anything for her equity. I know there is a deal here. Help!

Mentor: OK, let's take this step-by-step. Tell me about her motivation to sell.

You: She was living with her boyfriend who was helping to make the payment each month. But six months ago they split up. She struggled to make the payments for a few months, then she just couldn't do it anymore. She's three payments behind now and you have all the other financial details I submitted through the Mentorship student's Web site. She said if I don't buy it, she'll let it go back to the bank.

Mentor: Do you remember from the home-study materials about the strategy of buying subject to the existing financing?

You: I remember some of it.

Mentor: Tell me what you remember because this is how I'm going to coach you to buy this house. The best part is that you'll be able to do it with nothing down and very little risk.

You: Well, it means I buy the property but don't pay off her loan. I just have her deed me the property and make up her back payments, then each month I just send in the payment to her lender. Is that right?

Mentor: Yes. She deeds you the house for a token payment up front. Usually, we'll use ten dollars. Strange as it seems, for this to be legally binding, you need to pay something. It's called *consideration,* which is just a fancy legal term that means you gave her something of value to make the contract binding. You then clean up the property and start marketing it. Chances are, you'll be able to sell the house either on a rent-to-own basis or on an owner carry (see Chapter 8) and collect $8,000 to $20,000 up front, depending on whether you sell it or rent-to-own it. Then using your new buyer's money, you'll send in the back payments to the lender along with a letter explaining this is to bring this specific loan current. Each month after that, you'll send in the payment to her lender with the loan number on the check.

Top Five Benefits of Buying "Subject To"

1. You'll make money up front from your buyer, which you'll use to bring the loan current and pay yourself back for the minor fix-up you did.
2. You'll make a monthly cash flow.
3. You'll get all the tax benefits because you'll own the property.
4. You'll earn extra profit as the principal balance on the loan pays down each month (*amortization*).
5. You'll get a big check on the back end of the deal when your buyer or tenant-buyer cashes you out.

Going back into our coaching session . . .

You: Can I really do this? It sounds too good to be true. Is this legal?

Mentor: That's a really common question. The answer is yes; this is a perfectly legitimate way to buy property. For years, savvy investors have been using this method to intelligently buy properties and make a lot of money doing it. In fact, I've used this buying strategy myself on more than 75 houses over the past 9 years and it's made me wealthy. Still, there are risks you need to be aware of—you must look out for yourself in the deal.

You: I've heard there's something called a due-on-sale clause, which means if I bought the house like this, then the lender would call the loan "due in full."

Mentor: That's right. The lender has the right granted in the deed of trust or mortgage securing this loan to call it due in full if the house is sold without getting cashed out. But the due-on-sale clause, which is the biggest reason investors are leery of using this buying strategy, is really a paper tiger.

Due-on-Sale Clause Not a Big Problem

Just about every loan written for the past 20 to 30 years contains a due-on-sale clause. According to this clause, if a borrower sells the property without paying off the loan, the lender has the right to accelerate that loan and call it due in full within 30 days.

Here's what the technical language typically sounds like:

If title to the property described herein, or any interest therein, is transferred without the Lender's prior written permission, the Lender may declare all sums secured by this agreement immediately due and payable.

Sounds tough, doesn't it? But the due-on-sale clause is more intimidation than substance. Banks don't like borrowers to sell without the new borrower *assuming* the loan (and paying points, loan fees, etc.) or obtaining a new loan (paying loan costs, potentially higher interest, and starting the amortization of the loan from scratch!).

Interestingly enough, *Black's Law Dictionary* defines a due-on-sale clause as a "device for preventing the subsequent purchasers from assuming loans with lower than market interest rates." However, would a bank call a 15 percent loan due when the current market rates were 8 percent? Probably not. But if the loan is at 8 percent and the market rate is 15 percent, you can bet your local lender would just love to call the loan due just to force you to refinance the property at a higher interest rate. (The banker figures that even if you refinance the property with a different bank, at least you would have to cash out its old loan, giving it more money to lend at a higher interest rate.)

So banks are not in business to accelerate loans unless either you flaunt it (i.e., you make it overt that you bought the house without paying the loan off) or the interest rates have jumped dramatically.

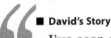

■ David's Story

I've seen a lot of investors miss out on huge profits because they just don't understand how far banks will go *not* to foreclose on a property. Banks don't want to own real estate; banks don't want to have bad loans on their books. They simply want people to pay them on time and take care of the house. When you understand this, you recognize how much power you have when negotiating with lenders to find creative solutions to help sellers solve their problems. The key is to *communicate* with the lender about what you need to make this work for its best interest, which is to have the loan brought current.

Many times, I have a three-way call involving me, the seller, and the lender. The seller introduces me to the lender as "a friend who knows more about this real estate thing than I do and who is helping me understand what exactly is going on and how I can make sure you get your money."

Then I take over and find out the specific details and exact status of the loan. Many times, I negotiate a payment plan known as a *forbearance agreement* with the lender right there on the phone. One word of caution: Don't tell the lender you're buying the property because the lender will resist your buying it without paying off or assuming the loan. If the lender asks any questions about who you are (which almost never happens), simply repeat that you are a friend of the seller.   ■

Negotiating a Forbearance Agreement

While talking with the lender before buying the property subject to the existing financing, work out a payment plan with the lender that helps you spread out the amount of money owed in back payments over time, or even better, adds the back payments onto the principal balance of the loan. This payment plan or workout is known as a forbearance agreement.

Remember, you're negotiating with the lender on the seller's behalf and not as a new investor looking to buy the property. Getting the seller's permission to do this is easy. You can hold a three-way phone conversation with the lender or just get written permission from the seller to allow the lender to discuss the matter with you.

From the lender's point of view, there are two main issues to work through:

1. How soon you can start making the current and future monthly payments
2. How you propose to pay the past-due amount (the payments in arrears)

In general, most lenders are more concerned with the monthly payments starting up and with the stability of these future payments than with when the past due amount will be paid. As a creative investor, you have lots of options. For example, you could negotiate to:

- Start making monthly payments now, delay for three or six months the other money owed (arrears), then make it up in one or several payments.
- Pay the arrears over time (3, 6, 12, or 18 months) while making the monthly payment from here on.
- Get a moratorium on any payments for several months (explaining to the lender why the seller needs this period of time and why things will be securely different at that future date).
- Add the arrears to the principal balance and start immediately to make the monthly payments. (This is sometimes called *recasting* the loan—adding the back payments to the loan and restarting it.)
- Make up the back payments in one payment with monthly payments to begin in 30 days.

Make sure you get the lender to acknowledge in writing any agreement for a workout plan. Never rely on an oral agreement. And don't send money to the lender until you have conducted all your due diligence (see Chapter 6).

You've Bought It "Subject to"—Now What?

One of the best parts of buying a house "subject to" the existing financing is that it opens up so many options for your exit strategy for the property. (We'll be going into detail on these different exit strategies in Chapters 7 and 8.) These options include:

- Hold and rent it.
- Immediately resell the property to a retail buyer.

- Wholesale the house to another investor.
- Rehab and resell the house to a retail buyer.
- Sell on a rent-to-own basis.
- Sell on a wraparound mortgage or land contract.

■ Peter's Story

One of the real estate agents I work with met a motivated seller at a baseball-card show. The seller was one payment behind on his mortgage on a four-unit building. I agreed to pay the seller $119,000, of which 3 percent was in cash to cover my agent's commission and the balance was me taking over the property subject to the seller's existing first and second mortgages. I also agreed to make up the month's back payment on the first and second mortgages and to make payments on them each month thereafter. I kept the building as a rental and four years later sold it for an $80,000 profit. ■

Three Biggest Questions about Buying "Subject To"

1. How will the seller get a new loan if this loan stays in her name and appears on her credit record? This can be a potential sticking point with a seller. But most lenders will credit the seller with having made the full payment as long as you can show them proof the loan has been paid for 12 plus months (e.g., canceled checks, etc.) and that the property has been sold (copy of the purchase agreement).

In some cases, the new lender won't give a 100 percent credit for the payments but rather only a 75 percent to 80 percent credit just as if the property were being rented out on a long-term basis. In this case, it may have some effect on the seller getting a new loan. As long as the seller has the income to make up for this and his income-to-debt ratios are in line with the lender's requirements, this won't be a problem.

Also, most people you buy from using this strategy are in foreclosure for a reason—they can't make the payments. Their need to solve this problem is a hundredfold more important to them than getting another loan down the road. Besides, if they lose the house to foreclosure, they'll have an even tougher time getting a loan later on because their credit will be trashed. This way, you save the seller's credit by bringing the loan current and making timely payments each month after that.

2. Who gets the tax write-offs? The person whose name is on the title. That is *you* the investor. Or if you *resold* the property on either a land contract or wraparound mortgage, then *your buyer* would get the write-offs.

3. What if the seller doesn't want her name on the loan forever? Negotiate for the longest time possible, then use a clause such as the following in your purchase contract:

> *Buyer agrees to pay off the Seller's loan(s) described above in this agreement within ____ months of closing of title. This clause shall survive the closing of title.*

Short-Term "Subject to" Rehabbing

As you may know from reading *Making Big Money Investing in Real Estate,* we're not big on recommending rehab projects. Here's why: We see people start investing with the idea to buy an ugly house, fix it up, then resell it. But invariably they forget to factor in the *real* costs involved with a rehab project—financially, timewise, and emotionally.

The Real Costs of a Rehab Project

- *The financial cost.* Most investors do factor in this cost up front. However, many find that once they start doing the work, hidden repairs eat into their profits.
- *The time cost.* It's easy to forget to factor in the intense month or two of work to get the house rehabbed and back on the market. This is especially important if you do some or all of the work yourself, rather than hiring outside contractors. Make sure the profit in the deal is worth all the time and energy you put in.
- *The emotional cost.* This is the cost most investors fail to calculate. Having thousands of dollars at stake for a two- or three-month period can create stress, especially if you don't have the financial cushion to cover additional rehab costs or a slow resale market.

A Smarter Way to Fund a Rehab

If you do plan to buy foreclosures, rehab and then sell them at retail prices, here is a better way to structure your deals. If you use this strategy, you will limit your risks and lower the amount of up-front money you put into the deal.

Imagine you find a seller who has a dumpy house in a nice part of town. The house needs serious repairs—about $30,000 worth—but once they're complete, the house will be worth $330,000. The seller is four months behind on the $210,000 first mortgage, which has monthly payments of $1,800, and agrees to sell you the house for $230,000.

You could put 20 percent down ($46,000) and get a loan for the remaining $184,000. In this case, you'd still need $30,000 cash for the repairs. If you did this, you'd net around $36,000. This would give you a return on investment (ROI) on your $83,500 of 43 percent—not bad, especially when you consider you made that return over a three- to four-month period (see Figure 3.2).

FIGURE 3.2   Traditional Way to Fund a Rehab

After-repair value (ARV) of house	$330,000
Your price	$230,000
Needed repairs	($ 30,000)
Closing costs (when buying)	($ 2,500)
Loan costs	($ 4,000)
Holding costs	($ 5,000)
Closing costs (when selling)	($ 2,500)
Realtor commission (when selling)	($ 20,000)
Net profit	**$ 36,000**
Down payment	$ 46,000
Closing costs (buying)	$ 2,500
Holding costs	$ 5,000
Repair costs	$ 30,000
Total cash invested	**$ 83,500**

Net profit ÷ cash invested = ROI
$36,000 ÷ $83,500 = 43% ROI (in a 3- to 4-month period)

However, we suggest you buy the house for a price of $230,000 subject to the seller's first mortgage of $210,000. . . . You'd then immediately make up the $8,000 of back payments to reinstate the loan and get started on the $30,000 worth of repairs. You'd agree to give the seller his money out of your profits when you resell the newly rehabbed house to a retail buyer.

The seller wins because he not only stops the foreclosure, but he also receives money within 90 to 120 days. (Notice that we switched to 90 to 120 days instead of three to four months. The change in terms makes the seller feel like he gets his cash faster—in *days* not months.)

We call this strategy of structuring the deal a *short-term subject to rehab.* Its main benefit is that it allows you to reduce the cash you need up front to approximately $45,000. This is not only $38,500 less cash needed up front—pushing your ROI to 89 per-

---

FIGURE 3.3 A Better Way to Fund Your Rehab—Short-Term "Subject to" Financing

---

After-repair value (ARV) of house	$330,000
Your price	$230,000
Existing first mortgage taking subject to	($210,000)
Needed repairs	($ 30,000)
Closing costs (when buying)	($ 2,500)
Holding costs	($ 5,000)
Closing costs (when selling)	($ 2,500)
Realtor commission (when selling)	($ 20,000)
Net profit	**$ 40,000**
Back payments made up on seller's existing mortgage	$ 8,000
Closing costs (when buying)	$ 2,500
Holding costs	$ 5,000
Repair costs	$ 30,000
Total cash invested	**$ 45,500**

Net Profit ÷ Cash Invested = ROI
$40,000 ÷ $45,500 = 90% ROI (in a 3- to 4-month period)

---

cent—but it means you won't need to get bank financing for the other $184,000 to make this deal work! (See Figure 3.3.)

This saves you many hours of getting your loan application and paperwork together and dramatically lowers your risk in this deal. It also saves you about $4,000 in loan costs for the money you'd have had to borrow if you didn't buy the house subject to the existing financing.

■ **Peter's Story**

One of the first foreclosure deals I ever did was a junker of a house I bought for $9,500 subject to the seller's financing. I didn't make a ton of money on it, but I still have a photograph of the house on the wall of my office because after buying this house, I really *felt* like an investor.   ■

Wholesaling or "Flipping" Deals for Quick Cash Profits

In the world of real estate investing, if a deal doesn't fit what the investor is looking for, then it's usually passed by. Once you understand how to keep your radar screen open to finding deals that don't fit your investing strategy but that you can wholesale to other investors, you'll make thousands of dollars more each and every year.

Most investors look only for deals that fit into their limited view of how they buy and sell properties. For example, if an investor buys foreclosures that need fixing up and then resells these properties to a retail buyer, he develops tunnel vision in his search for this type of deal. This tunnel vision can cause him to completely miss out on the chance to buy a foreclosure subject to existing financing or turning the property into a long-term rental. This can be costly because for every single deal that meets this one-track investor's criteria, five other deals slip by. This investor loses potential profits forever, simply because he wasn't open to other approaches.

While it's important to create a niche with your investing and develop a cookie-cutter process you can repeat within this niche, we also know the most successful investors profit from the deals they spot, even if these deals aren't ones they keep for themselves.

Imagine you were just starting out in the fishing industry. You bought a boat and spent your days putting out your nets and hauling in tuna. But one day when you come back into port, you notice that the boat docked next to you is selling a type of fish you've never seen sold before. The captain says that it's called yellowfish and that, while he never understood why people liked it, he'd found a few local restaurants that bought these fish at a healthy profit. In fact, he tells you he doesn't even specialize in catching yellowfish; they just end up in his nets while he's looking for tuna.

Over the next few weeks, you notice you've been hauling in many of these yellowfish while fishing for tuna. You think. Rather than throwing these fish back into the ocean (what you have been doing since you got started), why not sell them to local restaurants too. So that day, you put the yellowfish you catch into a separate cooler. When you get back to shore, you talk with four local restaurant owners who agree to buy your catch. You're amazed at how easy it was. In fact, you made such good money with such little extra effort that you start to cultivate relationships with more restaurants so you'll always have ready buyers for these yellowfish.

You can do exactly the same thing in your foreclosure investing. It's called *wholesaling* or *flipping deals*—when you take a deal you've contracted with a seller for and sell your rights under that contract to a third party. This third party, often another investor, pays you a cash fee to assign your interest under that contract over to him. He then buys the house from the seller. It's like taking the yellowfish you didn't want and selling them to another person for a quick cash profit.

Just like the fisherman looking for tuna, you might be looking primarily for sellers in preforeclosure who will let you make up a few months' back payments and deed you the house subject to their existing financing. Your plan calls for you to hold on to these houses for ten years or more. But you keep coming across sellers in foreclosure who just want to dump their houses. They aren't willing to sell their homes to you subject to, but they have lots of equity and are willing to give you a great cash price. You see that these houses (the yellowfish) will need a big rehab effort and you aren't interested in doing the work. But, still, you paid for the marketing that got these sellers to call you and you invested your time to meet with them, so you decide to flip these deals. You negotiate the best deals you can, then find other investors to buy the deals from you for a cash fee.

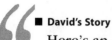

■ **David's Story**

Here's an example of a wholesale deal that Byron, one of the coaches in our Mentorship program, did a few months back. He found a seller who owned a fourplex that needed some cosmetic fixing. The seller, a referral from another seller Byron had worked with, was five payments behind and headed for foreclosure. Although Byron met with the seller and locked up a great deal, he didn't want to keep it for himself, doing the repairs and managing the fourplex. Instead, he sold his rights under the purchase contract to another investor for an assignment fee of $15,000.

The seller got a fair solution that included stopping the foreclosure and making $13,000 when the investor closed on the house. The investor who bought the deal got a great price and terms on a solid rental property in an area where he was already building his portfolio. And Byron made $15,000 for five hours of time invested. It was a win-win-win transaction. ■

So the next time you find a deal that doesn't meet your buying criteria, negotiate the best deal you can (whether for a cash sale or a subject to deal or some other strategy) and sign it up. Even if you don't want to keep the deal, try to flip it to a third party for a fast cash profit. (See Chapter 7 for details on how to flip properties.)

■ **Peter's Story**

I picked up a contract on a house in need of a total rehab. I looked at all that necessary work and said, "There's no way I'm going to spend the next two months fixing it up." So I sold my contract for $1,500. All totaled, I spent less than ten hours of my time on the deal. That meant I earned more than $150 an hour. Considering I was still working as an auto mechanic for a lot less money at the time I did the deal, that money helped me change my self-image. I could see my time being worth so much more than I was getting trading dollars for hours in the garage. ■

Short Sales: Making Big Money on Houses with Little or No Equity

When you are investing in foreclosures, you'll likely run into sellers who have little or no equity in their properties. You might think that if they have no equity, you can't help them. In fact, when most investors look at a deal in which the property has no equity and the existing financing payments are too high to cover by putting a tenant into the property (which rules out buying subject to the existing financing), they pass on the deal because they don't see any way to structure it and still make a conservative profit for their time, effort, and risk.

But there is a way—called a *short sale*—that lets you to take many of these no-equity deals and turn a fair, fast, and healthy profit on them. In a short sale, you negotiate with lenders to take less than what they're owed as full payment on a loan. For example, a lender has a $200,000 first mortgage on a house in foreclosure and is willing to accept $147,000 as full payment on the loan.

Why would lenders take less than they're owed? It's because of all the *real* costs they face when they're forced to foreclose on a property. First, a lender may lose money when it forecloses on a house. Foreclosure costs include attorney's fees, staff time, court or legal process fees, plus the huge discount that auctioned properties sell at.

Next, a lender may know the house's condition has severely deteriorated since the time it made the original loan, so the property may be financed over the "as is" value.

Finally, lenders face strict federal regulations regarding the ratio of bad loans they have on their books and the amount of money that must be kept in liquid reserves to balance this. With all these painful consequences of having to foreclose, it's no surprise that many lenders are willing to take a short sale to quickly solve an otherwise drawn-out process.

■ Peter's Story

Cheryl, one of the real estate coaches in our Mentorship program, received a call from a motivated seller in response to a postcard and flyer she had mailed him. The seller had spent $15,000 rehabbing the house, which he did all wrong. Then his wife got laid off from her job and they were losing the house to foreclosure. The house was worth $120,000 and had two mortgages on it—a first for $75,000 and a second for $8,000. The seller agreed to sell it to Cheryl for $50,000 provided she could get his two lenders to accept a short sale in that total amount. She contacted the lenders and sent them the ugly photos of the property, her repair list and bids, the low comps for the house, and the seller's financial information. They had their Realtor come out and do a broker's price opinion (BPO).

When the negotiations with the lenders were over, the first mortgage holder accepted a short sale in the amount of $49,000 and the second mortgage holder accepted a short sale in the amount of $5,000. Both lenders made their acceptance of her short sale offer contingent on Cheryl getting them their money within 21 days. She immediately got on the phone to three private lenders she worked with and borrowed the money to buy the property and make the needed repairs. Cheryl refinanced the property and pulled $20,000 out of it. She currently has the house on the market to sell it on a rent-to-own basis for $140,000.   ■

Best Situations for Short Sales

Here is a list of the most common situations in which short sales are appropriate. Note: The loan(s) *must* be in default or the lender(s) will not accept a short sale.

- Situations in which the property in foreclosure is financed so high that the lender stands to lose a significant amount of money if the house goes to auction.

- Situations in which the physical condition of the property has deteriorated so badly that only an investor would buy it at an auction and command a steep discount in price before bidding on it.
- Situations in which a large second mortgage is at risk because the first mortgage holder is foreclosing, allowing you to negotiate a short sale on the second mortgage.
- Situations in which your networking contacts tell you a specific lender has too many "nonperforming assets" on the books (i.e., too many bad loans) and you find a foreclosure property with a lien owed to this lender.
- Situations in which there's a mortgage from a private party (e.g., a seller-financed note) who would be willing to take a significant discount in the amount owed just to end the emotional nightmare of the foreclosure.
- Situations in which the seller has some other type of lien or private debt that's in danger of either being wiped out by the impending foreclosure or going unpaid because of the seller's financial distress.

Next, let's look at the specific steps to close a short sale.

Six Steps to Close a Short Sale

Step One: Lock Up the Property under Contract

Your first step in any short sale (indeed, your first step in any real estate deal) is to identify and meet with a motivated seller to lock up the property under contract before you spend time working with a lender to accept a short sale. If you need the short sale to make the deal profitable for you, make sure you insert a clause in your purchase contract with the seller specifically stating your agreement is contingent on the lender accepting a short sale. That way, you can build in enough profit in the deal to make it worth your time.

Here's what the legalese version of this clause reads like:

This agreement is subject to Buyer negotiating a short sale with the existing lien holders that will allow Buyer to pay no more than $_____ [the purchase price you are willing to pay which is less than the total owed] *total for the property. Seller acknowledges that he or she shall get NONE of the proceeds from the sale of this property other than the original deposit of $1.* [This final sentence is important because lenders will not accept a short sale if the borrower is making any profit from the sale.]

Step Two: Get Written Permission to Discuss the Loan with the Lender

Lenders won't talk with third parties unless the borrower (property owner) has signed a document expressly authorizing the lender to discuss the matter. The Authorization to Release Information (see Figure 3.4) should be faxed over to the lender as soon as possible. Typically, it takes a few days to get the authorization to discuss the loan into the lender's computer system.

Step Three: Call Lender to Open Negotiations

When you call up the seller's lender, ask to speak with the Loss Mitigation Department, which is the name of the department that deals with houses in foreclosure or preforeclosure. Be sure to reach someone who has the expertise and authority to help you.

Here's a sample script of your first call to the lender:

Investor: Is this the Loss Mitigation Department?
Lender: Yes, it is.
Investor: Great, then this is the department that handles short sales?

FIGURE 3.4 Sample Authorization to Release Information Form

AUTHORIZATION TO RELEASE INFORMATION

Authorization dated _____

Borrower: _____

Property: _____

     Regarding loan number: _____

To: _____
     (Lender's Name)

     _____
     (Lender's Address)

     _____
     (Lender's City, State, Zip)

     _____
     (Lender's Phone Number)

I (We) hereby authorize you to release information regarding the above referenced loans to _____ _____ (Authorized Party) and/or agents/assigns. This authorization or a copy of it may be sent via facsimile transmission and be fully valid and binding. This authorization is a continuing authorization for said persons or company to receive information about my (our) loan including duplicates of any notices sent to me (us) regarding my (our) loan. In addition I (we) hereby authorize you to discuss any aspect of our loan with Authorized Party.

_____ _____ _____
Borrower   Date of Birth   Social Security Number

Lender: Yes, we do. May I help you?

Investor: I hope so. My name is Peter. Who am I talking with?

Lender: Liz, I'm the department administrator.

Investor: I'm very glad to meet you, Liz. I was hoping you could help me with a small matter. What needs to happen for your company to accept a short sale on a defaulted loan?

Listen carefully as the lender tells you the specific criteria you'll need to meet before this lender will accept a short sale. Each lender requires a slightly different process before accepting a short sale. Some require the borrower to go to a credit counselor first before they'll even discuss a short sale. Others require you send them a written proposal and signed contract with a seller before they'll discuss a short sale. Still others will let you negotiate the short sale right over the telephone, provided you have faxed your Authorization to Release Information. Be sure to play by the lender's rules. In fact, many lenders will fax or mail you a written outline of their specific guidelines for a short sale if you ask them.

Six Tips When Working with Lenders on a Short Sale

While every lender follows different procedures, these powerful tips will help you successfully negotiate a short sale:

1. Keep a detailed log of all the calls and letters listing the date, time, who you spoke with, what you discussed, and any important details you'll need later. You will always be in a stronger negotiating position if you can reference the exact history of your conversations with a lender.
2. Make sure you're dealing with the *real* lender and not a "loan-servicing" company.
3. Be sure you're negotiating with the person who has the authority to say yes. Ask if that person is able to accept the short sale or if someone else will have to make that decision.
4. Respond to *all* the lender's calls and letters. Lenders in this department are used to working with borrowers who hide and ignore their correspondence. You can build a really strong relationship from which to negotiate a winning deal by consistently communicating with the lenders.

5. Gently remind lenders of their *real* costs to foreclose on properties. The best way is by asking questions to draw out what hassles and expenses they face if they have to foreclose, take the property back, and resell it. (See the sample script later in this chapter.)

6. As a last resort, hint at or openly discuss the "BIG B"—bankruptcy. When the lender learns that the borrower might be forced to declare bankruptcy if you can't work out a short sale, the lender just might have a change of heart.

Step Four: Send In Your Short-Sale Packet

If you need to send something in writing to the lender as part of your negotiation of the short sale, take the time to turn the packet into a tool to help you get a great deal. Here are the pieces to your successful short-sale packet:

- *Cover letter.* This letter gives the overview of what's included in the packet and why you are sending it. Highlight the condition of the house (if it's in bad shape), the seller's treatment of the house (if it looks like the seller has stopped caring for the house), and the slow market for this type of property (if it's a slow market in your area for this type of home). Also emphasize how your offer will provide a quick solution, allowing the lender to get cashed out in 30 days (or faster if possible). Finally, emphasize the *real* costs to the lender of having to go through the cumbersome and expensive foreclosure process.

- *Purchase agreement.* This is the contract that says the seller agrees to sell you the property subject to the lender accepting a short sale on the amount owed. Be sure that this agreement specifically states the seller will receive no money from the sale. *Lenders will not accept a short sale if the seller is making any money.*

- *Low comparables.* Include some printed statements of what other comparable homes are selling for. Obviously, you'll select the low comparables, not the high ones. If there aren't any low comparables, skip this item.
- *List of repairs needed and high-grade bids.* This list of repairs should be as extensive as possible and include the highest authentic bids you can get to have repair work done. Total this list and bring the message home to the lender that the property is in rough shape.
- *Ugly photos.* Take the ugliest photos of the property you can get and include enlarged copies of these photos. This helps the lender "get" the facts of your list of repairs in an emotional way. If the house is in great shape, which is rare with foreclosures but it does happen, skip the photos and list of repairs.
- *Credibility factors (use only if they will help build your case).* If you've done short sales before, include reference letters from lenders and past homeowners. If you have good credit or lots of cash, send proof of this to support your ability to perform on your offer should the lender accept. Examples include preapproval letters from other lenders for the short-sale amount, financial statements, and credit reports.
- *Hardship letter from the seller.* This letter should be either in the seller's own handwriting or on her stationery. The seller must explain why she can't afford the loan anymore and all the tough situations she's experiencing. You may have to help coach your seller to write an effective letter.
- *Net sheet (HUD-1).* This is the draft of the settlement statement that shows the lender the exact money to be received from the closing if your short-sale proposal is accepted.
- *Financial information on seller.* The lender often wants to see the real financial condition of the seller. This means you'll need to include copies of the seller's prior two years' tax returns, W-2s, a financial statement, etc. The lender wants to make sure the seller clearly can't afford to pay the loan.

- *Your offer to lender.* Finally, include your formal short-sale offer to the lender. Be sure to state your offer is available for a limited duration of time and explain why you feel you can only offer this amount of money and still conservatively make a profit.

Three Criteria of Irresistible Short-Sale Offers

1. *Fast* and *sure* closing—their most important criterion. No 60- or 90-day escrows; they want to finish the deal in 30 days or less.

■ **David's Story**

Not long ago, my mom and stepdad negotiated their first short sale. The house right next to the one they live in had been empty for more than a year. There had been a big fire and the house was only partially fixed up. After several weeks of trying to find the right people to even make their offer to, my mom and stepdad found the woman who had inherited the property after the old owners had died. This new owner lived quite a distance from the property. Two more months of legwork and my mom finally got the loss mitigation department on the phone. The house had a loan on it for approximately $120,000. The lender agreed to a short sale in the amount of $87,000. There was one catch: the lender said it would need that money within seven days—which they did! They rehabbed it and moved into it. Soon after, they decided to sell the old house they owned right next door. The moral to the story isn't that if my mom can do a short sale, you can too (although it could be). The bottom line is that you'll need to be ready to close fast; the lender just wants to get the deal over with.   ■

2. Cash *only*! Lenders won't finance a short sale for you.
3. No contingencies. Lenders will be leery of short-sale offers that have so many weasel clauses, they look like Swiss cheese. One easy way around this is to use a *liquidated damages* clause to give you a pain-free, covert way to walk from the deal if worst came to worst. (In *Making Big Money Investing in Real Estate*, we discussed liquidated damages clauses on pages 95–96 and 147–49.)

Step Five: Follow Up with Lender on the Phone

Once you have delivered your short-sale packet to the lender, don't sit back and wait for the lender to call you. Take the initiative to politely but doggedly follow up on your offer. Use each call as a chance to build rapport with the people in the lender's office and prod the deal one step closer to completion.

Once the lender accepts your offer, move to step six.

If your offer gets turned down, this is a great chance to negotiate a deal. But before you rush in with a higher offer, pose the following question:

> *I understand that our offer just wasn't a fit for you. You've all been so nice about the whole thing that even if I can't get my partner to offer more, I want you to know how much I appreciate your help and professionalism. Just so I can talk with my partner about this, what's the minimum our offer would have to be for your company to even consider it?*

Insider Secret: Never raise the amount of money you've offered until the other side has given you a counteroffer. This allows you to take whatever the lender says as a counteroffer and use that as an entry point to negotiate a lower price. While you might not be able to get the lender to give you a definite number the decision makers would accept, usually you can get them to give you a ballpark figure that you'd have to be close to for the lender to "even consider" your offer. This is just as good as the lender giving you a definite number for your negotiating purposes.

Step Six: Close on the House

Whether you are going to close on the house yourself or flip the deal to another investor, the final step is for you to cash the lender out and buy the house. Make sure if you plan to flip the deal to someone else that you have a backup plan in place if this investor doesn't come through. Make sure you honor your word with the seller and the lender.

■ **Peter's Story**

I received an e-mail from one of our students in Salt Lake City. Nick had been working for a pharmaceutical company until two months ago when he quit to go into investing full-time. At the time, Nick had done five deals and still owned three of the houses. He found a motivated seller who was two months behind on the payments on a beautiful two-story house. Originally, Nick structured the deal so he would net $20,000. But after listening to David's radio show, *Real Estate Radio* (<www.davidradio.com>), he learned about short sales. Nick talked with the lenders again and found out that the first and second mortgages were with the same company. After using the ideas from the radio show, Nick got the lender to accept a short sale. All totaled, Nick netted more than $110,000.   ■

Use this powerful strategy when the seller has little or no equity, or even when you want to increase your profits in an ordinary foreclosure deal. You can build in your profit by solving the lender's need while solving the seller's problem, too.

Leveraging the Power of "Subject to" with Discounting Debt

One reason it's critical to master buying with the subject-to-existing-financing strategy is because you can combine it with other buying strategies such as discounting debt.

For example, imagine you met with a seller who's three months behind on her two mortgages. The seller owns a three-bedroom house in a working-class neighborhood. The house needs some minor cosmetic work—new carpet and paint—for it to be worth $280,000. The financial details are as follows:

Loan information:

1st Mortgage of $210,000 at 6.75% interest with PITI payments of $1,500/month

2nd Mortgage of $45,000 at 12.9% interest with PI payments of $650/month

Cost to reinstate mortgages:

1st Mortgage: $5,000
2nd Mortgage: $2,200

Market conditions:

After-repair value of house	$280,000
Cost of minor cosmetic repairs	$ 4,000
Market rental value	$ 1,700/month

If you were to analyze whether it would make sense for you to bring both loans current and purchase this house subject to the existing first and second mortgages, you'd probably decide that the high-interest-rate second mortgage creates a negative-cash-flow situation. It just wouldn't be worth doing if you left both loans in place.

Here's how we would coach you to structure this deal:

1. Connect with the seller and find out why she's having problems making the payments. After talking with her using the

Instant Offer System (see Chapter 5), you would discover that she has a gambling problem and is having major financial problems in other areas of her life. When you ask her what she would really like to see happen, she answers that she just wants to walk away from the house with a few thousand dollars and start fresh somewhere else. You negotiate for a while, determining that if she sold it herself and factored in closing costs, real estate commission, back payments, and cosmetic fix-up work, she would probably owe money at the closing. At this point, the seller sighs and says that she just wants to walk away from the whole thing and be done with this nightmare.

2. We coach you to sign up the deal. You agree to make up the back payments, buy the house, and take over the property subject to the first and second mortgages. You create one very important contingency in the deal, though: You make sure the seller understands and agrees that the only way you're willing to move forward is if you can negotiate with the second mortgage holder to take a discounted cash payoff for the amount of money owed. Earlier, you learned that this strategy is called a short sale. Notice that you're looking to short only the second mortgage and not the low-interest-rate first mortgage that you want to keep in place.

3. Get on the phone and call the second mortgage holder. After getting the facts on the table (e.g., the seller has a gambling problem and won't be able to pay the first or the second mortgage; the seller may have to declare bankruptcy; the house needs some fix-up work before it will even sell; etc.), we put an offer on the table for the second mortgage holder. Here's how that negotiation could go:

   Investor: Of course, you could always just move forward and foreclose on the owner. Some lenders don't care about the fact that they wouldn't get much of anything after they factored in the costs to foreclose and have some investor pick up the property at a low cash price. The good thing is that we don't think this owner is the type of person who would get angry with the world and rip apart the house before the sale, just to spite you. I mean, you never know, but my gut says she's a pretty straight person. Anyway, in order to make this deal work for us, about the most we could give you for your note would be $5,000, maybe a little bit more.

Second mortgage holder: There's no way I could get my bank to accept such a low offer. You would have to do much better than that.

Investor: Boy, I can sure understand that. If I were you, I might just say, "To heck with getting any money at all, let's just foreclose to teach the owner a lesson." So I can understand that, from your view, you would need to get more money. I'm just trying to see if we can find a fit where I would even want to choose this deal over some of the other houses I'm looking at. And who knows, maybe we'll find that we just can't find a fit here. If that turns out to be the case, I want you to know that I'll be OK with that and that I really appreciate your time and openness to try to find a win-win fit here. What would be the lowest amount you could take to make this acceptable to your bank, knowing that it still needs to be low enough to work for us as investors?

Second mortgage holder: I don't see how we could accept less than $10,000 for the note.

Investor: Really [*scrunching up your face to get the right tonality of incredulity and disappointment*], the lowest you could take is $8,000 to 10,000? [Notice you just used the range technique here.]

Second mortgage holder: Well, we might take as little as $9,000 . . . but we'd need to have it in certified funds within 21 days.

Together we just negotiated a $36,000 discount off the second mortgage! This is pure profit for you in the deal. But wait, you say, you don't have that much cash to put in the deal. After you add up the $4,000 of cosmetic fix-up, the $5,000 to bring the first mortgage current, $2,000 in closing costs, and the $9,000 to pay off the second mortgage, that totals $20,000. You just don't have that kind of money. That's a challenge, but it's not insurmountable. Just like we don't put money into deals we do on a joint-venture basis with our Mentorship students, we're not going to send you a check for the $20,000 either! But soon we'll share several powerful techniques to cultivate sources of funding for your deals.

Let's get clear on your motivation to find the $20,000 to fund this deal. You will be getting a house that you'll have permanent, long-term financing in place at 6.75 percent interest. After you subtract all the costs, you'll have an instant equity position based on the $280,000 value of $47,000 *and* the house will generate a positive cash flow of at least $200 a month. Have we tapped into your greed glands deeply enough to spark you into finding a way to fund this deal?

Here are six ways to fund this deal (some you've read about, some you will come across later in this book):

1. Sell the house with owner financing, collecting a 10 percent down payment. This will get you $28,000 cash up front plus a great monthly cash flow and a large back-end profit.
2. Get a cash advance on one or more credit cards to fund the deal and then sell the house outright to a retail buyer.
3. Use your own money to fund this deal, knowing the profit will ensure a very high return on investment.
4. Borrow the money from a private lender and pay a fair rate of return on that money with the interest to accrue so you can protect your cash flow.
5. Partner with another investor who will put up the money and you'll split the profits.

6. Wholesale the deal to another investor for $10,000 cash.

Are you getting into the spirit here? The key to remember is that if the deal is good enough, you will find the money. You were able to take a deal that many investors just wouldn't have the skill to make work and turn it into a huge moneymaker for yourself by combining subject to financing with discounting the debt owed.

Many investors look only for properties with lots of equity. You've already learned how to make a healthy profit by using the short-sale technique. Here is another way to use that technique to make even more money. The next time you review the title report on a property you're buying and find any liens against the property you weren't aware of, don't panic. You just might have a great opportunity to make more money by buying those other liens for pennies on the dollar.

■ **David's Story**

I was helping a Mentorship student structure a deal on a $250,000 house that was in preforeclosure. The seller owed roughly $180,000 and wanted to get enough money from the sale to pay off $40,000 in debt that he had. Most were medical bills from a health situation several months back. I recommended that the student sign up the deal agreeing that she would make up the $8,000 of back payments and buy the property subject to the first mortgage of $180,000. The student would also agree to satisfy all the other outstanding hospital bills the seller had accumulated.

I then recommended the student get written permission from the seller to negotiate the outstanding bill with the hospital. I felt that the student could get that $40,000 of debt settled for as little as $10,000 to $15,000 *and* could work out a payment plan with the bank to pay that money over the course of 12 to 36 months.   ■

In this case, dealing with the seller's bills meant an extra $25,000 to $30,000 of profit, made in a way that allowed the seller to win, too. What other types of liens against the property can you discount? Remember, don't just think about debt as money owed to a lender on a mortgage. You can negotiate discounts on just about any lien against the property or, as you saw in the previous example, you can also negotiate bills the seller has that aren't even technically liens against the property and *still* get the seller to give you full credit for that money as if you'd paid the seller the face value of the debt.

You can discount things such as:

- Mechanics' liens for work done on a house
- Personal judgments against a homeowner
- Personal debts (e.g., medical bills, credit-card debt)
- Business debts

Here are two key considerations to help determine if the lien holder will accept less than what's owed:

1. How unsure of collection is the creditor? How likely (or unlikely) is the creditor of actually getting any money from the debtor? Is there a lot of equity protecting the lien? Or is the lien likely to get completely wiped out in a foreclosure sale? Maybe the debt isn't even secured against the property, in which case the creditor will probably be even more willing to discount deeper. Is it a first mortgage (in the most secure position and therefore the hardest to discount) or is it in third position after two mortgages? You get the idea here. The more the debt is at risk, the deeper the discount you should go after.

2. How badly does the creditor need the money? Obviously, a roofer whose cash-flow situation is tight will be more likely to give you a discount than a large mortgage lender. So find out as much as you can about the people who are owed the money.

■ **Peter's Story**

I always ask the sellers not only what they owe against the property, but *who* they owe it to. I have found that private parties are much more willing to take significantly less than what they're owed just to get their money fast. That's why I love buying properties where the prior seller carried back a large first or second mortgage; many times, they're willing to discount this note if the current seller is behind in payments. Never underestimate the power of "cash now." I don't even think it's about greed on the prior seller's part; it's much more about relief. They just want to be able to get a clean break from that house they thought they had sold years ago.   ■

Imagine you found a seller who had a $360,000 house and was $10,000 behind on the first mortgage of $320,000. Also, there were two liens against the property: a mechanic's lien for $18,000 for the new roof and $15,000 owed to an ex-husband as part of a divorce settlement.

First, you call the roofer to see what you can do:

> *Ring, ring . . .*
> *Roofer:* Hello
> *Investor:* Hi, this is Ian, is Ralph there?
> *Roofer:* This is Ralph. What can I do for you?
> *Investor:* Oh great. It sounds like I caught you in the middle of something?
> *Roofer:* No, I was just organizing things for my next job. What can I do for you?
> *Investor:* Actually, I was calling because I'm an investor who sometimes buys notes and liens that look like they'll be wiped out in a pending foreclosure or bankruptcy. I'm sure you probably knew about how the Sutton Street house you have a mechanic's lien on is about to be foreclosed on any day now. It looks like you aren't the only one the owner didn't pay. I don't know if there's any reason for us to be talking or not

about my buying your lien for a cash payment. You probably wouldn't even want to talk to me about my handing you a cashier's check in the next 14 to 30 days for your outstanding bill on that property, huh?

Roofer: You mean you'd pay me cash for that lien? Why would you want to do that?

Investor: Well, it wouldn't be because I'm just a nice person. I mean, I am a nice person but I want to be clear here that's not why I would get you cash, if I decided it would even work for me. Like I said, I'm an investor who buys liens and notes that look like they are about to be foreclosed out and then I aggressively go after making money from the note. The way I figure it, I know that if I get a big enough discount in exchange for getting someone like yourself a cash payment, then the big gamble I'm taking pays off for me on enough of these things that I make a nice living doing this. But boy, you probably wouldn't even want to talk about selling your note for a discount, huh?

Roofer: Yes, I would. How much would you give me for the note?

Investor: To be frank, I'm not even sure if I want to buy this note or not. May I ask you a few questions to see if this is even a note that I would want to buy?

Roofer: Sure, I'd be glad to answer any questions. [*Notice how the conversation has turned and you, the investor, are in the driver's seat where you belong. Now it's time to build the lien holder's motivation to sell.*]

Investor: What have you done to collect on this note in the past?

Roofer: We tried invoicing the owner for about two months. And I went over to the property to collect the money three times myself.

Investor: And that worked [*big eyes*]?

Roofer: No, he wouldn't even open the door and talk with me.

Investor: Really? Tell me about what that was like? [*Voice getting softer and using scrunchy face*]

Roofer: I was so pissed off at the guy. I mean, I took three guys off another job to fit in the roof on his house and then he stiffs me. I started banging on the door and he shouts out that he's called the cops on me. I just took off.

Investor: What did you do then to collect?

Roofer: I filed the paperwork for the mechanic's lien and I figure he'll have to pay me someday.

Investor: How does that mechanic's lien thing work? Does it mean he has to pay you off in 30 days or something [*big eyes*]?

Roofer: No, basically it means it's a lien against the property so before he sells it, he'll have to get me to sign off on some papers or he can't sell it. So he'll have to pay me plus interest before I'll sign.

Investor: That makes sense . . . And so if the bank moves ahead with the foreclosure, he'll just pay you at the foreclosure sale?

Roofer: No, if it goes to foreclosure, I probably won't get paid at all. I'd have to take him to court and get a judgment for what he owes me and then try to collect on that.

Investor: Oh, OK. Well, I'm not sure if this is a lien I'm going to want. It sounds like the chances of collecting are less than I originally anticipated. If I were willing to buy the lien from you for cash, what would you even do with the money?

Roofer: The money would be going back into my business, which had to cover our costs for the roof. I had to pay for the guys and most of the materials. I still kick myself for not getting a larger deposit up front from the guy.

Investor: Well, at least you're lucky enough to have your business going so well that you don't really need the money. It just may be your better option to sit tight and hope he makes good on the ten grand he owes the bank in late payments, and then in a year or two, he may refinance the property and pay you off or something, right?

Roofer: Doubtful. He's the kind of jerk who would end up losing the house to the bank. How much are you willing to pay me for the lien?

Investor: Oh, well, I'm not sure if I would want to buy it or not yet. I mean if you wanted some huge amount of money like $7,000 or $10,000 for the lien, then obviously that wouldn't work for me. What's the least you would take for the lien, knowing that this would have to work for you, but it would also have to work for me as an investor taking a mighty big risk here? $700? $1,000? Or maybe a little bit more?

Roofer: I'd never sell it for that little; it just wouldn't be worth it. I'd need to get at least $5,000 for it.

Investor: Really [*scrunchy face*]. $3,000 to $5,000 is the least you'd take? [*Range technique*] Are you sure you couldn't go lower?

Roofer: No, I wouldn't take any less.

And away you go. You just got the note for $3,000 and were able to pocket the other $15,000 as extra equity that goes along with your purchase of the house. The call probably took you 20 minutes tops. Where else can you make $15,000 in 20 minutes on the phone?

But wait, you're not done yet. You still have that $15,000 owed to the ex-husband! If you follow the previous ideas, you'll probably be able to buy that note for even less. Why? Because the ex-spouse likely never expects to get paid that money anyway. She probably lives out of state and she'll be thrilled to get any money you pay now and get closure to the situation. You might even get the note for as little as $500 to $1,500, which would make you another $13,500 to $14,500 on the house the moment you buy it.

Now do you understand why notes and liens and judgments can often be a great profit center for you in a foreclosure deal? Savvy investors know that the more little liens and private debt a seller owes often means more profit for the investor.

You negotiate with the seller as if these debts couldn't be discounted and were at face value, but you know you can get them for pennies on the dollar later by negotiating directly with the creditor.

■ **Peter's Story**

I recently got an e-mail from Paul, one of our students. Paul owns a cleaning business and one of his employees was losing her $60,000 home to foreclosure. She had a first mortgage for $13,000 and a second mortgage for $25,000 and owed $2,000 to a local hospital. All together, Paul was looking at buying the house for $40,000. He went ahead and talked with the second mortgage holder and offered the decision makers $7,000 for the note. They countered him at $9,000. Paul went back and asked them to meet him in the middle at $8,000. They agreed. Next, he called up the hospital administrators and offered them $500 for their bill. After having their board review the offer, they accepted. All totaled, Paul went on to have a positive cash flow by renting the house for three years before selling it for a $30,000 net profit. Over the past four years, Paul has built up a net worth of a million dollars and a monthly cash flow of $10,000 from his investment activities.   ■

Why Every Investor Can Be a Cash Buyer

Many investors mistakenly believe the only way you can buy with cash is by having perfect credit for borrowing money or by having the liquid cash sitting in a bank for them to tap into. We hope you've already seen that this just isn't true. You've learned about subject to financing, flipping deals, and discounting liens. You've learned that sometimes you can get the seller some or all of his equity out in cash and buy subject to the seller's loan. And you've learned about flipping deals that get the seller cash—and get you cash too! Now it's time to learn the seven sources for funding your deals, listed in the order you prefer to tap into them.

Seven Sources of Funding for Deals Other Than Your Local Bank

This is listed in the order of desirability for you, the investor.

Source One: The Seller

The single best source for you to fund the deal is the seller. We know this might sound strange. After all, isn't the seller so financially strapped that he can't even make his monthly payment? Well, yes, but remember the seller has existing financing in place, and in some cases has equity in the house to lend you.

You've heard of using other people's money (OPM). Now understand the true power of OPM (other people's mortgages). That's what "subject to" financing really is—using other people's mortgages to make you wealthy.

This isn't complicated; subject to financing is the seller being your bank, at least functionally. And the seller is even more obviously your source of funding when he agrees to take a note for part or all of the money you have agreed to from your purchase of the property.

Source Two: Your Buyer

Depending on how you plan to sell the property, you can generate immediate cash to fund your deal from a few thousand dollars to hundreds of thousands of dollars. You'll find many more details on how to make this part of the deal work in Chapters 7 and 8, but for the moment, it's important to understand that your buyer can be a great source of funding for your deals.

If you sell the property on a rent-to-own basis, you can typically collect 3 percent to 5 percent of the purchase price as a non-refundable option payment. If you are selling with owner financing (e.g., land contract, wraparound mortgage, All-Inclusive Trust Deed [AITD]—all explained in Chapter 8), you can typically collect 10 percent to 15 percent down. And if you structure the deal in which your buyer brings in a new first mortgage, then you can generally get *all* the money you need to fund a cash purchase of the property from your motivated seller who was in foreclosure.

Let's look closely at this final way to structure a deal in which you'll be using your buyer's money to fund your way into the deal. Let's start with an example.

Imagine you meet a motivated seller who is in foreclosure and about four weeks from losing her house at auction. She owns a four-bedroom, two-and-a-half-bath house in a nice part of town. The seller admits she has been living in denial for the past five months and now finally realizes something has to happen fast.

The house, worth $300,000, is in great shape; all you have to do to get it in showing condition is to have it professionally cleaned. It has an existing first mortgage of $180,000. You meet with the seller and, using the simple five-step system in Chapter 5, negotiate an all-cash price of $220,000, with you paying all closing costs. You feel great about negotiating a price that's $80,000 below market value, but you're scared about where you'll get the $220,000.

Here's one way to make this deal happen. You resell the property *before* you close on it with the seller. That is, you put it on the market for $280,000 and offer to help your buyer finance the purchase. Have your buyer get a 90-5-5 loan, which means that person brings in a new loan for 90 percent of the purchase price ($252,000) and puts 5 percent down ($14,000). You carry back a 5 percent second mortgage ($14,000).

It's a win-win-win solution. Your buyer, who probably has less-than-perfect credit, wins by both saving $20,000 on the price and having your help on the financing. Your seller both saves her credit and salvages $40,000 of equity. Best of all, she will never have to look back again. And here's what you'd make on this deal:

Purchase price	$220,000
Selling price	$280,000
Gross profit	**$ 60,000**

Look at what you net and when you get that money:

Gross profit	$60,000
Closing costs	($ 3,000)
Cleanup	($ 500)
Advertising	($ 500)
Net profit	**$56,000**

All totaled, you'd net $56,000 on the deal. You'd get $42,000 cash at the closing in the form of a check you'll get from the title or escrow company. And you'd have a second mortgage for the other $14,000.

In this example, your buyer is making you 12 percent interest-only payments on that note with a balloon note due for the $14,000 in three years. That means each month you collect a check for $140 and in three years your buyer will give you a lump-sum payment of $14,000–cash your buyer will most likely get by refinancing the house.

You'll learn more about how to quickly sell houses like this in Chapter 7, but for now, understand that you *can* handle this deal—an all-cash deal—without any cash or credit of your own. In real estate, you get paid for the specialized knowledge you bring to a deal. That knowledge lets you do things most sellers don't have the expertise to do and most Realtors don't have the experience or comfort level to do.

Isn't it reasonable that once you get good at this game, you'll be able to find someone who wants to buy a nice house for $20,000 below value, especially when you are willing to participate in the financing to make the deal work?

You can also use your buyer's money to fund your way into a deal in which you need to get the seller a small down payment. Because you can sell the house with owner financing and typically collect 10 percent down, you can often get the seller a chunk of money for his equity and buy the property just subject to the existing financing. The seller gets all the cash he expected from the deal up front; the buyer gets a house with no bank hassles; you make a healthy profit for being the matchmaker between the two parties.

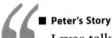

■ **Peter's Story**

I was talking with Marcia, one of our Mentorship students from five years ago. Marcia told me about a deal she made with a motivated seller who called her after seeing a small classified ad she ran. The seller was $1,500 behind on his $35,000 mortgage. Marcia bought his house subject to the existing financing and used the $5,000 option payment she collected from her tenant-buyer to pay for the back payments and for the other $1,500 the deal cost her. Marcia still owns that house, which generates a $200 positive cash flow each month. It's an example of funding the deal with her buyer's money.   ■

Source Three: Your Money or Lines of Credit

If the amount of money you need is small enough that you can comfortably fund the deal, and if the deal is good enough to warrant putting your own money into the deal, then seize the opportunity.

Here are two considerations to take into account before funding deals yourself:

1. Is the amount of money you're putting into the deal small enough that you feel comfortable taking the risk of losing it? If the answer is no, look for a different source of funding.

2. Are you experienced enough investing that you feel comfortable putting more of your money or credit on the line to fund the deal? If you've paid your dues, invested in your real estate education, and completed some deals, then you're qualified to put your own money or credit on the line. Remember, sometimes having money or available access through your lines of credit to money is a detriment to your creation of wealth. Easy access to money can often make early deals too easy to obtain. If they were harder to fund, you might decide to pass on the deals altogether. You cannot make up for a lack of knowledge and experience with money and *not* expect to pay a healthy price for learning that lesson.

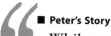

■ Peter's Story

While reading through postings on our Mentorship student Web site, I came across one from Byron, one of our coaches. In his posting, he gave his formula for how much to discount the money you pay to a seller when you have to make up back payments on a house you're buying subject to the existing financing. His formula was to lower the money paid for the house by $3 to $4 for each $1 you have to put into the deal up front to catch up the back payments. Therefore, if you put $5,000 into the deal to catch up the back payments, Byron recommends you get at least a $15,000 to $20,000 discount off the purchase price of the house. I looked back over the deals I had bought subject to and recognized that I followed his formula most of the time. And the times I didn't, I regretted it.   ■

With that cautionary point made, we think that many times it does make sense for you to fund your own deals, especially when you're talking about making up some back payments and taking over subject to the existing financing. Here are three sources of cash open to many investors:

1. *Credit cards.* Cash advances are a fast source of cash.
2. *Home equity loans.* Smart investors set up these lines of tax-deductible credit before they need them.
3. *Pension plans.* Many 401(k) plans allow you to borrow money from the plan and repay it later, paying interest into your tax-deferred plan. Self-directed IRAs are also great vehicles for investing in real estate, especially Roth IRAs.

Source Four: Private Lenders

By private lenders, we don't mean banks or hard moneylenders. Rather, we recommend starting to cultivate relationships with people who can fund deals for you in exchange for your paying them a fair interest rate on their money.

Here is a list of people you can approach about funding deals for you:

- Family
- Friends
- People on fixed incomes who need greater returns than CDs and money-market accounts can give them
- Other investors who deal in real estate and are willing to get a fair return on a first or second mortgage (Note: The people you want for good rates will almost always want a first mortgage with good equity protecting them.)

Imagine you are talking with a family friend about your investing. You know this person has retired and is living fairly comfortably on his investments. He could be a potential private lender for your real estate business. Here's a script of what to say to a potential private lender:

Potential private lender: So you have been investing in foreclosures for how long now?

Investor: Well, it's been about seven months now since I got started. Funny enough, it all started from a book I picked up while browsing in the bookstore.

Potential private lender: How's it been going so far?

Investor: I'm really pleased with the way things have been going. I've done four deals so far. The first deal I found was a foreclosure that I flipped to another investor. The deal was good, but I was a bit scared to fully commit to the deal. I got $12,000 for assigning this other investor my contract to purchase the property. He closed on the house and rehabbed it and resold it two months later and made $43,000. The next two houses I still have. And the last deal I picked up three weeks ago. I'm in the final stages of fixing it up and then will sell it to a retail buyer. I expect to make around $30,000 on that one.

Potential private lender: Wow! That's great. I'm really happy for you.

Investor: Yeah, in fact the more deals I do, the more I realize that the only thing slowing me down is needing to cultivate private lenders who want to fund a deal where there's plenty of security in it for them and a fair rate of return on their money. Hey, maybe you know someone who has some money in a CD or in a money-market account who would like to earn a healthy rate of return secured by a first mortgage on a house with at least 25 percent to 30 percent equity protecting the loan?

Potential private lender: Actually, I might be interested in funding a deal if it really was secure enough for me. What interest rate would you give me?

Investor: May I ask you a question first? [Softer tone and voice now] Why would you even want to fund a deal?

Potential private lender: With interest rates where they're at, I'm only getting 5½ percent on my 12-month CDs. If you can give me a higher interest rate and it's really a safe investment, then I'd like to get a better rate of return.

Investor: That makes sense. What type of interest rate did you hope to make?

Potential private lender: I don't know—8 percent to 10 percent would be great.

Investor: OK, actually that's about what I thought would be fair to pay a private lender for using their money to fund a deal . . .

See how easy that was? Don't try to sell private lenders on some high rate of return. Let them tell you what interest rate they think would be fair. You'll be shocked at how many will mention a number that's well below what you might have volunteered before reading this book.

Here are the top four concerns of private lenders:

1. Security
2. Security
3. Security
4. Reasonable interest rate and security (they tied for fourth place!)

We hope this drives the point home. Many investors make the mistake of approaching individuals they know about funding a deal, then trying to sell this potential private lender on a high rate of return on their money, or on the ease of the transaction. Neither of these is important to private lenders. They want to make sure their investment is safe. That's why high rates of interest actually scare private lenders away. After all, they say, if the investor is willing to pay 15 percent interest, this deal must be risky.

So speak to the private lender's fear of losing money first, second, third, and fourth! This means conveying three things:

1. Assurance that you've done this before. It's difficult to get money from a private lender (other than "love money" from family members) unless you have successfully done a few deals. The better your track record, the safer your private lender feels.

2. An understanding of what's protecting him in the deal. Make sure you show the prospective private lender the appraisal on the property or comparable homes that sold to substantiate the equity that will protect his loan. Let him know he'll be protected—just as a bank is with a recorded mortgage or deed of trust. Encourage him to take all the paperwork to his attorney for review to make sure it's all on the up-and-up. Show him actual photos of the house, or better yet, take him to the house and talk him through your plans while walking through it.

3. Show private lenders your exit strategy on paper, including your detailed financial analysis of how you plan to make enough from the deal to pay back their money. (This document is called a pro forma analysis.)

You might be saying, "This sounds like a lot of work," and you'd be correct. It *is* a lot of work. The advantage is that once you help these private lenders make money once, they'll start to trust you and your next deal will be much easier. In fact, if you treat your private investors right, and this means *never, ever* letting them lose money, they will tell their friends and associates about you. This could mean you'll never struggle to fund a deal again. It may take you 12 to 18 months to get to this point, but it's worth it.

■ David's Story

I received an e-mail from Paul, a student who had bought a home-study course we offer on buying homes subject to the existing financing. Paul bumped into a motivated seller in a 7-Eleven store. This seller had a rental property he needed to sell fast. The house was worth $170,000 and the seller owed $73,000 on a first mortgage plus $24,000 of back payments. Paul signed up the deal subject to the existing financing using the forms from our course. He borrowed $40,000 from a private lender to pay the back payments on the house and fund the fix-up work it needed. (His private lender was his mother-in-law who got tired of losing money in the stock market!) Paul still has the house as a rental property, which generates $800 a month of positive cash flow. He currently has $42,000 of equity in the house. One year ago, Paul took the leap and left his job with the federal government to go into investing full-time. He's never looked back.   ■

Source Five: Money Partners

In addition to finding people to lend money in exchange for a guaranteed interest rate, you can find other investors who would like to partner on a deal. They provide the funding for the deal—either by putting in their own money or by borrowing the money based on their credit and income—and you put in the work. You then "split" the deal.

You can split deals in many ways. You could joint-venture on the house on a 50-50 basis. You can split money with any proceeds from the sale of the house first going to repay the cash investment of the money partner, then with 25 percent of the net profit going to your money partner and 75 percent going to you. You can structure the deal any way that wins for both of you.

Four Things to Be Careful Of When You Bring In a Money Partner

1. *Put all the details in writing.* A clear written agreement is essential to creating a smooth business relationship. Your agreement should spell out the details of who is responsible for what parts of the deal, how you'll handle funding for the deal, how you'll split profits, and how to end the relationship if it doesn't work out.
2. *Be careful of a general partnership.* A general partnership, the default business relationship unless you set up another one, means each party is 100 percent responsible for all the liability, yet each party only gets a portion of the profit. Consider using a limited liability company or a limited partnership to lower your risk.
3. *Check references.* Always know whom you are doing business with. Have these partners lived up to their word in the past? How did they react to conflict and stressful times in the past?
4. *Make sure you have control or at least a recorded interest.* If the deal is for real, your partner should always be willing to have you record a *memorandum of agreement* to protect your interest (or if you are the one in control, then you should be willing to record something to protect your partner's interest).

Source Six: Hard Moneylenders

Imagine you find a great buy on a foreclosure house. The house in our example needs $40,000 of rehab work and has an after-repair value of $400,000. You negotiated well with the owner and locked up a price of $230,000. That's more than $100,000 of potential profit, even after you factor in holding costs, closing costs, and all the rest. (Heck, it's almost enough to make us want to take on the rehab project! Almost . . . We'd still probably sell the deal to another investor for a cash assignment fee, but that's just us.)

But you wonder, How can I get the $230,000 to buy the property, plus the money for closing costs, plus the $40,000 to rehab the property? Consider a source of financing called a *hard moneylender.* We know this term conjures up images of a loan shark with a muscle-bound companion ready to make you pay up or else, but that's not true at all. Hard moneylenders have a large pool of cash they're willing to lend to investors who are buying real estate in situations with enough equity in the properties that they consider the loans safe.

When you are borrowing from hard moneylenders, they won't care what your credit is like, or how much money you earn, or the size of your bank account. They only care about one thing—is there enough equity in the property to secure the loan? In fact, one benefit to hard money loans (beyond the obvious part of not having loan applications to fill out or credit reports pulled) is that often you won't have to personally guarantee the loan. The property itself will be the sole source of collateral of the loan, not your good credit. Of course, you'll have to pay some hefty costs to get this money.

Here are three things you pay a hard moneylender for the loan:

1. *Higher than market interest rates.* Most hard moneylenders will charge you 12 percent to 15 percent interest on the money you borrow.
2. *Points. Points* represent a fee you get charged up front for the loan. One point is equal to 1 percent of the loan amount. Typically, you'll have to pay a hard moneylender at least five to ten points up front for the loan. The only good news about points is that you can usually roll them into your loan so you can "pay" them with borrowed money.
3. *Prepayment penalty.* Hard moneylenders know that when they charge such high interest rates on the money they

lend, investors who borrow from them are highly motivated to either resell the property or refinance the property to pay off the high interest rate loan as quickly as possible. Hard moneylenders don't get all that available cash by being dumb; many put a prepayment penalty into the loan that says, "If you pay off the loan before a certain date, you have to pay up to six months' interest."

Let's look at what these costs mean in our current example. First, your hard moneylender will charge you five points on your $270,000 loan, which comes to $13,500. Plus you'll have $2,000 of closing costs, which your friendly neighborhood hard moneylender will let you add into the loan amount. Finally, you'll have to pay 15 percent interest on the property, which you got the hard moneylender to agree to let "accrue." This means you don't have to pay each month while you're rehabbing and reselling the property; the interest charges will simply be added to the principal balance you owe. Thankfully, you got away without having to pay a prepayment penalty.

Now you close on the house using $230,000 of the lender's money, plus a little more for closing costs, and get to work on the rehab. A hard moneylender isn't going to give you the whole $40,000 up front for the rehab work; that would put the lender in a bad position if you just took that money and didn't do any work. Instead, that money will be paid out to you (either through an escrow fund set up or directly from the hard moneylender) as you need it to pay for completed work or for materials needed to get a chunk of the work done.

Two months later, your rehab is complete. Congratulations! You put the house on the market. Because you want a fast sale, you list the house with a quality Realtor in your area for $399,980. Sixty-eight days later, you close with your buyer for $392,000. After you pay all your costs, you net more than $75,000. It took a lot of work on your part to coordinate all the contractors and keep your Realtor working fast to get the house sold, but in the end it was worth it. In fact, for years to come, every time you drive past that house, you'll get that warm fuzzy $75,000 feeling!

With all these costs, why wouldn't you just go to your local bank and get the decision makers to lend you the $270,000? Good question. The answer is that a conventional lender won't lend you money based on the after-repair value. In fact, a conventional lender won't lend you money based on the *market* value. A conventional lender will lend you money based on the current value or your purchase price—whichever is *lower.* This means even if you lock up a $100,000 price on a house that has a current "as is" value of $170,000, the lender will only lend you money based on the $100,000 purchase price. You lose the benefit of counting that $70,000 worth of equity as part of the consideration of whether the lender will lend to you or not.

We know this seems crazy but that's just the way it works. We didn't make the rules, which is one of the reasons we avoid working with conventional lenders when we can.

Hard moneylenders will make loans based on the "as is" value or based off the after-repair value, depending on what you arrange with them. Because they'll maintain a low enough "loan-to-value" ratio to protect themselves in case you default, they won't require a credit check or proof of income. You can actually get a hard money loan even if you went bankrupt four months ago and have been out of work for the past seven years!

What amount of equity will hard moneylenders require to protect themselves in this loan? Generally, they'll lend up to 70 percent or 75 percent loan-to-value. This means there will need to be at least 25 percent to 30 percent equity protecting the lender's loan.

Also, when borrowing from a hard moneylender, it will take 48 to 72 hours to cut you a cashier's check. Compare that to borrowing from your local bank, which can take up to 30 to 60 days to "rush" your loan through. When you're buying foreclosure property this far below market value, fast access to cash is everything.

■ David's Story

I got a call from my student Cheryl who said her Realtor located an REO property that Cheryl had a contract on to buy for $48,000. Because the ARV of the house was $95,000 and the house only needed $7,000 of repairs, I got excited for her. She asked if I wanted to fund the deal as a hard moneylender. Because I had made other loans to her in the past (not to mention having bought a dozen houses with her over the years), I agreed. The point is that sometimes successful investors make a great source of hard money loans.   ■

Source Seven: VA and HUD Foreclosures

One niche area of foreclosures is buying VA (Department of Veterans Affairs) and HUD (Department of Housing and Urban Development) foreclosures. These government agencies help people buy homes by guaranteeing loans to the lenders. In some cases, the borrowers default on the loan payments and the lenders foreclose. After the foreclosure process winds its way to completion, these agencies (VA and HUD) end up with the properties. They want to sell these properties as easily and quickly as possible, so many times they give investors with good credit and income great deals on price and terms.

Many of these properties end up with these agencies because the agencies offer programs that help buyers get into homes with low down payments and fairly loose credit standards. Both of these factors help increase the default rate of borrowers with these types of loans. It also means there isn't enough equity in the properties to entice investors to buy them at the foreclosure auction.

It's an established fact that the lower the amount of equity homeowners have, the higher the rate of default on their loans. It makes sense. The lower the equity a homeowner has, the less the person has at stake in the house and the higher the monthly payments will be (compared with a homeowner who has a lower loan balance and more equity).

Herein lies your opportunity. These agencies want to entice people to bid on their foreclosed houses. One way they do this (besides selling the house for a discount on what it is worth) is by agreeing to provide the financing needed to purchase one of these properties. Many times, they'll even let investors buy with as little as 5 percent down to cover all the closing costs. Considering that most investors need to put 20 percent to 25 percent down plus have cash to cover closing costs to secure traditional financing, this proposition can be appealing.

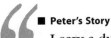

■ **Peter's Story**

I saw a duplex that was a HUD foreclosure advertised on the weekly HUD listing in my local paper. The vacant property was in an area I knew would be good for a rental. HUD provided 5 percent down financing for investors so I decided to bid on the property. My bid of $80,000 was accepted. Over the next ten years, I kept the property as a rental with a positive cash flow. Then I sold it for $245,000. I kick myself when I realize I could have bought five more just like that one. Learn from this mistake. Don't sit back and *think* about investing; get out there and do it.   ■

Be aware of the following downsides to these types of deals:

1. They require getting traditional bank loans. You'll need to have the credit and income to qualify for the financing (not to mention the hassle of dealing with the application process).

2. You have to purchase these properties *as is.* This means you need to clearly know the condition of the property you're buying. With most homes you buy, the sellers have certain

disclosure obligations; these agencies don't have to live up to the same standards.

3. You'll be limited on the number of these types of houses you can qualify for, using their financing. For some reason (possibly the statistically higher default ratio), these agencies will cut off your ability to buy using their financing after three to five houses. If you have the financial resources to take advantage of these programs, make sure you pick only the very best deals. You'd hate to look back and see a marginal house you bought keep you from buying a home run of a house because you couldn't find another source to fund the deal.

4. Sometimes the ease with which you can purchase these houses encourages investors to get lazy conducting their due diligence to make sure the deal is worthwhile.

Buying VA foreclosures can be a great entry point into investing or an added tool in your investing toolbox. But sometimes the easy ways of buying aren't the smartest. With the easy financing the VA provides (at least it's easy on the first three to five of the houses you buy; then it typically becomes much harder to get), you buy at a price that's higher than one you'd pay all cash for.

But wait. You say you didn't pay all cash, that you used the bank's money with 5 percent down to cover closing costs (e.g., Realtor commission, escrow fees, etc.). This is one of the biggest mistakes investors make when buying using traditional financing. They forget that when they personally sign on a loan, they are really cash buyers. And cash buyers should get a *big* discount for paying cash.

Again, wait. How can we say you're paying cash when you only have 5 percent down and most of that covers closing costs? Any time you're borrowing the money so the seller gets all of his cash at the closing (whether it's from your bank account or your lender's bank account), you're buying with cash. Don't think the money has to be all yours; the important point of view here is the seller's.

When the VA provides the financing, you'll have to personally sign on the loan. The VA is not going to let you sign on behalf of your corporation or limited liability company. Therefore, we believe you should consider VA purchases as all-cash sales. Remembering this will help keep you sharp and hungry when you're negotiating to get the right price up front.

■ **David's Story**

I will be the first to admit I've made mistakes when buying VA foreclosures. In fact, I remember one property I bought with a partner and ended up paying $25,000 too much for. After owning it for about a year, I sold it for an amount at breakeven to my costs. No matter what your Realtor thinks you should offer or how easy the financing is to obtain, make sure you're really buying low enough to make the deal a conservative moneymaker for you. That said, investors all have a few dogs in their buying past. The key is to lose *little* when you lose, to win *big* when you win, and to make sure you win a lot more than you lose.   ■

The best way to tap into these deals is to hook up with a Realtor in your area who specializes in these types of programs. If you ask around, you'll have no problem finding a Realtor to work with. It's up to you to train this agent about the criteria you have for the properties you want to buy. If you neglect to do this, your agent will show you every house on the Multiple Listing Service (MLS)—the proprietary database of properties for sale in an area. You don't have time to sort through all these properties. That's one of the reasons your agent makes a commission—by helping you narrow the search for properties.

Also be sure to make your own decisions on what price to offer. Many agents will say you can't offer such a low price and that you're crazy to try it. That's easy for them to say; not only do they have nothing to lose in the deal but they also make more money on the higher price you offer. (Do you recognize a conflict of interest?) Instead, use your agent to help you find the houses you want to make offers on, to help write up and present your offers, and to help you do the paperwork once your offer is accepted. Be certain to do your own negotiating, and never tell your agent how much you're actually willing to pay. Even agents with the best of intentions can inadvertently cost you thousands of dollars.

One Final Strategy to Structure the Deal

If you have decent credit and income to buy a foreclosure property at a good cash price, rather than take over the house subject to the existing financing, you could formally assume the financing that underlies the deal. We don't recommend it because you're much better off buying subject to. Still, it's an option you should keep in your toolbox. If you decide to formally assume the loan, take into account the downsides (compared to buying subject to). To summarize, the disadvantages are:

- *Increased risk.* The lender will make you sign personally on the loan.
- *Need for good credit and verifiable income.* The lender will make you fill out all the normal loan application documents you prefer to avoid.
- *Higher costs.* The lender will charge assumption costs ranging from $500 to a few thousand dollars.

You just learned 12 powerful strategies to structure your foreclosure deals no matter what the size of your bank account or the quality of your credit. (See Figure 3.5 for a review list.) Remember to consider all seven sources of funding the next time you negotiate

---

FIGURE 3.5   Review List of All 12 Buying Strategies

1. "Subject to" financing
2. Short-Term subject to rehabbing
3. Wholesaling or flipping
4. Short sales
5. Subject to financing with discounting of debt
6. Funding source: seller
7. Funding source: your buyer
8. Funding source: your money or lines of credit
9. Funding source: private lenders
10. Funding source: money partners
11. Funding source: hard moneylenders
12. Funding source: VA and HUD financing

---

a deal. Develop the confidence to know that if the deal is good enough, you'll always be able to fund the deal in some way.

You're better off to work only with sellers who are motivated to sell fast. In the next chapter, you'll learn almost two dozen techniques to find these types of motivated sellers.

22 Ways to Find Motivated Sellers

It's time to shift your focus onto exactly how to find foreclosure deals. You're about to learn some of the most powerful ways to create multiple streams of foreclosure deals into your investing business.

Before we get into the details of finding foreclosure deals, let's get clear on the outcome you're working toward. If you're investing part-time (between 10 and 20 hours a week), then your goal is to set up three independent lead sources, each yielding an average of one high-quality appointment with a motivated seller every week. If you are investing full-time (between 30 and 40 hours a week), then your goal is to create five independent lead sources, each yielding an average of one high-quality appointment with a motivated seller every week.

Many beginning investors—and some seasoned veterans for that matter—make the costly mistake of looking for "foreclosure deals." Don't look for foreclosure deals; look for motivated sellers. (Or better yet, use the ideas in this chapter to get them to look for you!)

When you focus on finding deals, you waste your time and energy on low-priority items. Instead, focus on the single highest-paid activity you have as an investor—connecting with motivated sellers who have compelling reasons to sell. These are people whose situations cause them to be flexible on either price or terms (ideally *both*!).

■ **David's Story**

At a recent workshop we were teaching on Purchase Option investing, one of my students talked about how he'd been looking for Purchase Option deals but couldn't find any. As he explained what actions he'd taken, it became clear he was looking for the wrong thing. He was seeking "lease-option deals" and "'subject to' deals" and "foreclosure deals." I urged him to let go of his search for "deals" and instead focus his efforts on consistently looking for and connecting with motivated sellers.   ■

When you meet with enough motivated sellers, you'll find great foreclosure deals, and great lease option deals, and great deals to flip to other investors. The deals—and the profits they bring you—are *by-products* of looking for and connecting with motivated sellers. Never lose sight of this critical distinction.

Let's dig into 22 different ways to find motivated sellers. Some of these techniques focus exclusively on the foreclosure market. Others will be more general in nature and yield motivated sellers who are not in foreclosure or preforeclosure. We didn't think you'd mind making money helping a tired landlord or an out-of-town owner even if he wasn't in financial distress. (For more information on how to work with sellers who aren't in foreclosure, read our previous book, *Making Big Money Investing in Real Estate.*)

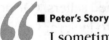

■ **Peter's Story**

I sometimes hear from starting investors that there aren't any motivated sellers in the area where they want to buy; that market is just too hot. In my experience, motivated sellers exist in *any* market. For example, take the San Francisco Bay Area, unarguably one of the hottest housing markets in the country for the past three years. I received an e-mail from Jim, a beginning investor, who read a favorable review of our last book by syndicated real estate columnist Robert Bruss and then bought it. Jim found a seller in foreclosure who lived two houses down from his girlfriend Candace's house in the Bay Area. Two weeks after Jim tried to contact the owner, *the owner called Jim* at Candace's home. It turns out that the seller's daughter and Candace's daughter both went to school together.

After negotiating back and forth, Jim and the seller agreed on a purchase price of $337,000 payable as follows: $27,000 cash to make up the seller's back payments, $70,000 to the seller with $20,000 of it up front, and the balance as an owner-carry note due down the road, and subject to the $240,000 existing financing. Jim and Candace scrambled to borrow the money from friends and family and were able to close on the house. After $20,000 of cosmetic work, the house was worth $550,000. Jim and Candace made more than $150,000 from their first foreclosure deal in a market others said was "too hot" for finding motivated sellers. The bottom line is that you can either stay with your story that you can't find motivated sellers where you live, or you can get to work and start making the profits by finding the motivated sellers who do live in your area.   ■

Making a Deal Work—Finding a Motivated Seller

All great deals start by finding a motivated seller. Motivated sellers have both an "M" and an "S."

"M" = motivation

"Motivation" is a compelling reason to sell the property and involves a limited time to find a solution, ideally within two months or less.

"S" = situation

"Situation" means either the seller has enough equity that she can significantly discount the price of the property, or the underlying financing is good enough that you might want to take over subject to the existing loan(s).

To find qualified sellers over the phone, be careful not to squander time with nonmotivated ones. Find out quickly if the seller has a situation that would lead to a sale. Only after you know that will you invest time to visit the property and discuss the owner's emotional and situational reasons for selling (which you'll learn in Chapter 5).

Script for Qualifying Sellers over the Phone

To be effective as an investor, learn how to qualify sellers who call you about one of your advertisements or mailing pieces. Look at the markers in the following sample script so you can understand *why* savvy investors ask certain questions *when* they do. The questions include cues about voice volume and inflections to use when following this script for calling back homeowners:

> *Ring, ring . . .*
> *Seller:* Hello?
> *Investor:* Hi, this is David. May I speak with Sophia?
> *Seller:* This is Sophia.
> *Investor:* Hi Sophia, you had given me a call a few hours ago about a property you had that you wanted to sell. It sounds like I caught you in the middle of something? [*Scrunching up your face and getting softer at the end to produce right tonality*]
> *Seller:* No, I was just helping my son with his homework.
> *Investor:* Oh, how old is your son? [*Building rapport*]
> *Seller:* He's nine.
> *Investor:* That's a fun age. Well, Sophia, can you tell me about your property?

Seller: It's a five-bedroom, three-bath house, on a half-acre lot up in the Prescott Hills subdivision——

Investor: [*Breaking in to get to your first real qualifying question fairly quickly*] Wow, this sounds like a wonderful property [*getting much softer now and scrunching up your face*]—why would you ever consider selling it?

Seller: My husband and I are getting a divorce and the payments are too much for me to afford by myself.

Investor: Oh, that's tough. [*She's motivated so now you are willing to invest the time to connect and really probe for more information to see if her situation will allow you to craft a win-win deal here*] What do you think the house is conservatively worth? [*When you say the word "conservatively," your tone should go down—just like you want the price to go down*]

Seller: Well, the one right down the street sold for $449,000 two months ago and it's roughly the same size as ours.

Investor: OK . . . and what is it that you owe against the property?

Seller: $380,000.

Investor: And is that all on one mortgage or is that spread out on two or more loans?

Seller: That's all on a first mortgage.

Investor: And the payments on that are . . . roughly . . .

Seller: About $2,700 a month.

Investor: Does that include your property taxes and insurance? Or do you pay that separately?

Seller: No, that's PITI, which is principal-interest-taxes-insurance.

Investor: Oh, OK . . . and is the house current or is it a bit behind in the payments? [*Notice you said "the house," not "the seller."*]

Seller: Actually, we're four months behind.

Investor: All right, and did you get any fancy letters from your lender saying it is going to start the foreclosure process?

Seller: It actually filed the Notice of Default three weeks ago.

Investor: How much did the lender say it was going to take to bring the property current?

Seller: $12,300.

Investor: OK. By the way, what school subject were you helping your son with? [*Once you get the tough numbers part done, it's a good idea to break the seller's sense of embarrassment or negativity and build a bit more rapport.*]

Seller: [*Laughs*] It was American history. He's got a test tomorrow and I was helping him get ready for it.

Investor: [*Laughing too*] Oh boy, I never did like history in school although I find it fascinating as an adult. Your son's really lucky to have a mom like you who is willing to make the time to work through his homework with him.

Seller: Well, I've always done my best to encourage him in school.

Investor: That's really important. Sophia, where were you planning to live once you've sold this place?

Seller: I'm moving in with my sister for a few months to figure things out. She's got a big house with two open rooms, one for me and one for Kevin.

Investor: That's great that she can be there to support you. A question for you, Sophia [*voice gets much softer and scrunch up your face*], If this house doesn't sell, what were you going to do then?

Seller: It's got to sell. I'll lower the price if I have to but it's got to sell. I know it will sell, even if I have to list it with a Realtor.

Investor: OK . . . and bottom line, if you could paint a perfect picture of what you wanted to happen, what would that be?

Seller: I just want this all to be over and to be able to walk away with at least $20,000.

Investor: Oh, OK. You just want this all to be over and for you to be able to walk away with $10,000 to $20,000 after all was said and done. Well, it sounds like something I may be interested in. Do you have your calendar handy so we can set a time to meet and for you to show me through the inside of the house?

Seller: Sure . . . .

For you to consistently find motivated sellers, you have to invest either time or money. You can invest your time by using techniques you are about to learn like *co-op advertising* or *networking.* Or you can pay other people we call *bird dogs* to find deals that you like. Or you can buy direct-response advertising that will get deals to come to you through *direct mail* or *classified advertising.*

Following are 22 techniques to find motivated sellers. Test out enough of these so you can settle on three to five that you can consistently apply. They will keep your "deal funnel" full each month.

Technique #1: "I Buy Houses" Classified Ads

One of the best ways to get motivated sellers to come to you is through classified advertising. A small ad in your local paper can generate several hot foreclosure leads each month (see Figure 4.1).

Even more important than what your ad says is where you place it. There are three places you should test your classified ad.

First, try your local daily paper. Place your ad in the Real Estate Wanted section. *Caution!* Some papers will try to move your ad off into the Real Estate Services section. This is bad news and will cost you big so make sure this doesn't happen to you.

FIGURE 4.1   Sample Classified Ad to Find Motivated Sellers

I Buy Houses—Cash!
Stop Foreclosure/Double Payments
No Commission/Fees
888-234-2233   x 63   Recorded Msg.

■ **Peter's Story**

I was on a coaching call with several of my Mentorship students
and we were discussing classified advertising to reach motivated
sellers. One of my students in Denver, Colorado, complained that
his classified ad in the *Denver Post* was too expensive. I asked a few
questions to help him determine if the ad was a worthwhile
investment for him. First, I asked him how much the ad cost him
each week and how many leads it generated over the course of an
entire month (the minimum amount of time you need to test your
ad). It turned out that he and his wife were paying over $125 a
week for the ad to run each Sunday in the Real Estate Wanted
section. On average, the ad generated six to eight calls a month;
only half of those were quality leads. Now this sounds like an
expensive way to generate leads, but note his answer to my next
question, which was, "How many deals did you close out of
those six to eight calls a month?" He said, "We've been running
the ad for eight weeks and so far we've gotten one deal from
the ad. We made about $25,000 from that deal." Not surprising,
he still runs that classified ad.   ■

Also run your classified ad in your local *Pennysaver* or *Thrifty
Nickel*-type paper. These free weekly publications are sent out
each week directly to each home in the area. These publications

vary in price and are the publications in which the average area resident will advertise a garage or moving sale. In these types of publications, you want to run your ad in the For Sale section. Also, see if you can spend an extra $20 to $40 to put a box around your ad. While this costs more, a box around your ad will almost always increase your response rate for it magnetically draws more eyes to your ad.

■ David's Story

I've been advertising in my local *Pennysaver* for the past five years. I spend an average of $2,500 a year on my ad. Now this might sound expensive; after all, it adds up to more than $12,000 paid over the past five years. But considering I've made over $250,000 from the property that ad has brought me, I know it's been one of the best advertising buys I've ever made.   ■

Third, place your "I Buy Houses" ad in specialty papers in your area. For example, if you have a military base nearby, test placing your ad in the papers that cater to the military personnel. You can also experiment with some of the smaller weekly papers in your area to see if they draw enough responses to be profitable for you. The bottom line is that you need to test these advertising opportunities and see what your results are.

Technique #2: "I Buy Houses" Signs

Dollar for dollar, your best lead source might be those corrugated plastic "I Buy Houses" signs that you place around your targeted area or neighborhood. These inexpensive signs are usually either 18 inches by 24 inches or 24 inches by 24 inches (see Figure 4.2). Over the past three years this technique has been one of the top three sources of deals for our Mentorship students across the country.

FIGURE 4.2   Sample "I Buy Houses" Signs

> # I Buy Houses—Cash!
> ### 888-234-1234   x 55

Or

> # I'll Buy Your House
> ### 7 Days or Less!
> ### 888-234-1234   x 56

Place these signs anywhere in your marketing area where cars are likely to be stopped long enough for the drivers to jot down your phone number. Effective locations include freeway on-ramps and off-ramps, stop signs, traffic lights, and across the street from busy parking lots. A word of caution: Local ordinances probably control sign use in your area so you'll have to investigate before you decide whether it's the right thing to do.

 ■ **David's Story**

First, I divide my local farm area into eight parts. Each week, I hire someone to put up signs in one of these eight parts, usually on wooden stakes I buy at Home Depot. I take care to make sure the person I hire doesn't get carried away putting up too many signs in any one area. I use a different sign made up in a different color (although it has the same phone number) the second time I put signs throughout my farm area. I've found this lowers the number of complaints I get and keeps me out of trouble with local sign authorities.   ■

One of our students in New Jersey, Marc, put out 30 of these signs as a test. He got a call from a motivated seller who was helping her mom, who had recently moved into a nursing home and wanted to sell her house. The house needed about $35,000 in repairs and Marc agreed with the seller on a price of $95,000. After the fix-up work was completed, the house was appraised at $235,000. Currently, Marc has a tenant-buyer living there, which is generating a $270 monthly cash flow.

Technique #3: Magnetic Car Signs

Considering that the average American drives more than 12,000 miles a year, not having magnetic "I Buy Houses" signs for both sides of your car means you're missing out on an easy way of generating leads. Depending on the type of car you drive, you might also want to get a third sign for the back of your car. In many cases, these are the most visible signs of all.

For example, a Mentorship student of ours had her Suburban painted with "I Buy Houses" signs. She got a call from a seller who was three payments behind on his mortgage. So far, she's made more than $20,000 on the deal and the numbers are still climbing.

We urge you to get these signs for your car, not just for the leads they can generate, but for the statement they make about you. We've had the chance to mentor thousands of investors getting started making money investing in real estate, and we've noticed that beginning investors have trouble seeing themselves as investors. Nothing works better to help new investors change their self-images than to publicize their businesses by having those "I Buy Houses" signs on their cars. The first few weeks or months can be awkward, but soon your self-image will expand to include this new part of yourself.

■ **David's Story**

I've had those tacky signs on the sides of my car for a few years now, long enough that they seem like part of the car. I've been amazed at the number of people who ask me questions about my investing business because they've seen the signs on my car. For example, I was at a gas station when a guy filling up his car asked me about how I buy houses. It turned out he had a house he was selling and asked if I'd take a look at it.   ■

Technique #4: Larger "I Buy Houses" Signs

If small signs work well, look for chances to graduate to larger advertising solutions. Possibilities include:

- Billboards
- Large signs on tax sale lots
- Bus bench ads
- Mobile signs (trucks and trailers)

■ **Peter's Story**

One of the coaches in our Mentoring program, Byron, told me how he and four other investors pooled resources and placed "We Buy Houses" ads in 20 well-positioned bus benches around Denver. Byron said each investor pays $125 a month and gets one-fifth of the leads the bench ads generate. Over three months, Byron has closed one deal from this cooperative advertising campaign—a quick flip that netted him $8,000.   ■

FIGURE 4.3   Sample Postcard to Find Motivated Sellers

Stop Foreclosure!
Get Money Now!
Save Your Credit!

We buy houses in any area or condition.
Here's your quick and easy solution:

✔ *FAST* Closing
✔ *INSTANT* Debt Relief
✔ *FREEDOM* From Aggressive Lenders
✔ *GUARANTEED* Written Offer Within 48 Hours
✔ *HARD-TO-SELL HOME?* No Problem!
✔ *NO EQUITY?* No Problem!
✔ *NO* Commissions

**Call 1-888-555-1212 x 12
toll-free 24-hr. Rec. Msg.**

Technique #5: Postcard Campaign

The simplest direct-mail campaign to find motivated sellers is to send "I Buy Houses" postcards to property owners in the beginning stages of foreclosure. (See Figure 4.3.) In most states, this will mean either a Notice of Default has been recorded against the property or that a foreclosure lawsuit has been filed and a lis pendens recorded against the property. (Chapter 2 explained the first steps of the official foreclosure process.)

How often should you mail your postcard? We recommend you experiment by sending this postcard once a week for three or four weeks to your list of Notice of Default or lis pendens properties.

We've received our best results printing this as an oversize postcard (8½ inches by 5½ inches). We use a bright canary-yellow or goldenrod card stock. We've found two benefits of using post-cards versus letters:

1. *You save money.* With postcards, there are no envelopes to purchase. You can even use a standard size postcard (3×5) and save significant postage.
2. *You save time.* There are no letters to fold and stuff, no envelopes to close. Also, with postcards, you won't hurt your response rate by using printed mailing labels (something we warn you about in a section that follows).

Why would anyone *ever* use a letter instead of a postcard? Because if you use a compelling letter sequence (examples follow), you'll get a higher response rate. It's more complicated to conduct a letter campaign, but it can be worth the effort. The only real way to know if it's worth the extra effort is to test both postcards and letters and see which is most effective for you.

How to Get a Default List for Free

You can get the Notice of Default list for free. Many investors subscribe to a local, regional, or national information source-provider company to get updated Notice of Default or lis pendens lists each week. This service is valuable, but given the choice between paying money and free, we're biased toward free!

To request these lists, call a local title company (you can find several in your yellow pages under "title company" or "title insur-ance company") and use the following script. Remember, a title company stands to make a hefty profit over the years by selling you title insurance or even performing an escrow function for your real estate closings.

Here's a script for talking with your title company:

> *Ring, ring . . .*
> *Title company rep:* Hello?
> *Investor:* Hi, this is David. I'm a new investor in the area. I'm interviewing a few title companies in the area to see who I want to start working with. Does your company work with investors who do more than one closing a year? [*Do you think you have the title company's interest yet?*]
> *Title company rep:* Yes, we do work with investors.
> *Investor:* Are you the person I should be speaking with or should I talk with someone else in your office?
> *Title company rep:* No, I'm the person you should be talking with. I'm one of the title company's sales reps.
> *Investor:* Oh, great. My name is David, what's your name?
> *Title company rep:* Alice.
> *Investor:* Hi, Alice. Like I mentioned earlier, I'm new to investing in the area and I'm just interviewing a few title companies to see which ones provide the services I'm looking for. Now, you can sell me title insurance, right?
> *Title company rep:* Yes, we work with a lot of investors in the area.
> *Investor:* Great. What other services do you provide to investors like myself? Are you able to get me out-of-town owners' lists and landlord lists?
> *Title company rep:* Absolutely. We can even print up mailing labels for them.
> *Investor:* Actually, I'd prefer to get them e-mailed to me in a spreadsheet. That way I can do my mailings on the computer. How often do you guys send out your foreclosure lists? [*Nothing like assuming the sale to get the answer you want to hear.*]
> *Title company rep:* We send them out weekly.

See how easy that is? Many title companies provide these mailing lists, which are easy for them to create on their in-house computer database as a value-added service to their best clients—investors like you.

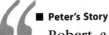

■ **Peter's Story**

Robert, a student in Nevada, found a motivated seller from a foreclosure list he obtained from his local title company. The seller had lost her job and then lost the financial help of her boyfriend and was headed straight toward foreclosure. Robert agreed to make the payments current on the $126,000 loan, which cost him $8,000, and take over making the payments. The house was worth $160,000 from day one. Currently, Robert has a tenant-buyer in the house, which makes him $500 a month. He will have a back-end profit of $25,000 when his tenant-buyer cashes him out of the property down the road.   ■

Technique #6: Sequenced Letter Campaign

A well-written letter sequence is one of your greatest tools for finding foreclosure deals. It works best to use a sequence of three to four letters, each of which builds on and refers back to the earlier letter. We use a three-letter sequence for mailings to properties on the Notice of Default and lis pendens lists. Figure 4.4 shows the first letter of that sequence.

We use four techniques to increase our success with this mailing campaign and we highly encourage you to use them as models.

First, we send the letter out in a simple envelope with the homeowner's name and address imprinted on the envelope and *not* on a mailing label. Because most people sort their mail over a trash bin, it's important that our letter look like a piece of personal mail and not junk mail.

FIGURE 4.4   First Letter of a Three-Letter Sequence to Homeowners in Default

---

Stop Foreclosure!
Get Money Now!
Save Your Credit!

Thursday, 10:15 AM

Dear Friend,

I remember one seller I talked with several months ago who was in the beginning stages of foreclosure.

He had called me up because a close friend of his told him about how I buy houses in the area.

He was scared. He was angry. He was embarrassed that his friends and family might find out about how he was about to lose his house to the bank. And he was uncertain of what to do next.

We spent about two hours together going over his situation and what all his options were. In the end he chose to sell me the house for a fair price.

I can't promise I'll be able to buy your house. As an investor I need to make a profit when I buy. But I CAN GUARANTEE that I will do my very best to lay out exactly what your options are and help you plan out what to do next.

I understand that when things get stressful, as they probably are for you right now, that the easiest thing to do is to try to put all the painful thoughts out of your mind. But ignoring the situation won't make it go away.

I know. Over the past several years I've worked with dozens of homeowners just like you who got caught in a trap not of their choosing.

Just like you they were good, hardworking folks. It's just that for one reason or another they got a step behind and from there they just never were able to catch a break. Has it ever seemed to you like when it rains it pours?

FIGURE 4.4   First Letter of a Three-Letter Sequence to Homeowners in Default (Continued)

I know that in my life when tough times came, they seemed to bring along as many other troubles as possible! I remember one time when things were so hard for me financially that I feared losing my house. I dreaded waking up in the morning and facing my sense of humiliation and thinking about how I let my family down.

Does this sound familiar?

The foreclosure clock is ticking. In just a short time, your home will be sold at public auction. Now is the time to figure out what to do about it.

Call my office to set up a free seven-minute phone consultation. It's free and confidential and comes with absolutely NO OBLIGA-TIONS of any kind.

We'll spend the time going through your situation and see if there is anything I can do to help. Again, while I can't promise I'll buy your house, I do **GUARANTEE** that I will listen and do my best to lay out all your other options so you can choose what's best for you.

Of course you're skeptical. That just proves you are a responsible person.

But what have you got to lose? The phone call is confidential and FREE.

Call my office right now while you're thinking about it. Just call 888-555-1212 x32 right now.

Sincerely,

John Investor

P.S. If you'd like, I can share with you several little-known ways to stall or even stop the foreclosure process when we talk on the phone. Just call 888-555-1212 x32 right now to set up your free and confidential phone consultation.

P.P.S. If you're in a big hurry to find a solution right away, call me on my cell phone at 777-555-3434.

Second, we use a live first-class stamp and not a metered frank. This helps the mailing piece look like an actual letter from a friend rather than a piece of junk mail.

Third, we use only our return address and not our company name. We do not want to give the homeowner any clue about whom the letter is from. This really creates an urge for homeowners to satisfy their curiosity about who sent them the letter. And the only way they can satisfy this urge is to open it up and read it.

Fourth, we mail these letters in a concentrated three-week period. We want this repetition so we can break through any feelings of denial the homeowner may be feeling. We mail our first letter of the sequence as soon as we get the address. Then we mail the second letter one week later, and the third letter one week after the second one. Again, each letter refers back to the earlier letter and builds in emotional power.

■ **David's Story**

One of our Mentorship students used exactly this letter sequence to put together a great deal. She got a call from a landlord-seller who lived two hours away from the foreclosed house. The house was about to be auctioned off two days later! The mortgage was for a total balance of $43,000 but our student got the lender to agree to accept the back payments of $4,000 to reinstate the loan. She then bought the house subject to the $43,000 mortgage. She also agreed to give the seller another $6,000 as a lump-sum payment due in full within 24 months of closing. The house is worth more than $75,000. And all this came from a letter mailed to a seller who was in default.   ■

Technique #7: Door Hangers and Door-to-Door Flyers

A variation on the direct-mail theme is to hire someone to put "I Buy Houses" door hangers or flyers at the houses in your farm area. The upside is the lower cost (from 8 to 18 cents a flyer) compared with the higher cost of sending letters. The downside is that you can't target your recipients like you can with your Notice of Default and lis pendens mailing campaigns. Still, this is a powerful tool to add to your marketing toolbox.

■ Peter's Story

One of our Mentorship students used this distributing-flyers technique and picked up a new house in a nice neighborhood. The owner, who had just moved to New Zealand, didn't care about the house anymore. He was in the preforeclosure stage and simply deeded the house to our student subject to the existing financing. Only $1 changed hands. All this came from simple flyers put out house by house for a third of the cost of mailing letters.   ■

Technique #8: Co-op Mailing Campaigns

You can use this technique to mail thousands of letters each month for free. It will take time for you to set up the necessary relationships, but co-op mailings are a way to tap into the power of direct mail, no matter what your financial situation.

Your goal is to find four other "partners" to go in on your mailing with you. They each pay one-fourth of the cost and get to include a one-page flyer or letter advertising their business. Make sure you choose four noncompetitive businesses that are complementary to your own investing business. For example, if you are mailing from a geographical list, which is a fancy way of saying a list of homes in a specific area or zip code, you have many prospective business owners to co-op with: restaurants, dry cleaners, real estate agents, etc., who want to be getting their marketing message into the hands of these people on a regular basis.

14 More Mailing Lists You Can Use to Find Motivated Sellers

In addition to geographic lists, you can mail to targeted lists such as:

1. Landlords
2. Out-of-town owners
3. Owners with delinquent taxes
4. Owners with mechanics' liens recorded against their properties
5. Homeowners with large private mortgages recorded against the house
6. Homeowners who bought on wraparound mortgages or All-Inclusive Trust Deeds (AITDs) or recorded land contracts
7. Military personnel who own houses and who are about to ship out
8. Notice of Default/lis pendens
9. People who just filed for divorce
10. Probate property lists
11. People who just filed for bankruptcy
12. Vacant-house owners
13. Building code–violation owners
14. Condemned-property owners

Insider Secret: Subscribe to your local legal notice newspaper. In it, you'll find the addresses of people in both the starting and advanced stages of foreclosure (see Figure 4.5). You'll also obtain valuable information on mechanics' liens filed, probate proceedings, or lawsuits that may give you the inside track to finding a profitable deal.

FIGURE 4.5   Sample Sections of the Legal Notices

Section 101: Notices of Default
1233122 Trustor: John and Susan Bond, Trustee: Fidelity Title, Beneficiary: U.S. Finance, Reinstate Amount: $2,410.00, Original Note: $24,500, T.S.FID-03-03345, Loan Yr-FileNo: 1998-203442
1298722 Trustor: Craig and Linda Jones, Trustee: CRC, Beneficiary: Countrywide Home Loans, Reinstate Amount: $7,960.00, Original Note: $305,000, T.S.02-17745, Loan Yr-FileNo: 2000-827762

Section 201: Notices of Trustee Sales
10:00 a.m. at the front steps of City Courthouse, 220 W. Broadway, San Diego. Property at 987 Windy Sea LN, Carlsbad, CA 92333. Sold by Cal Western 858/555-1200 Orig Loan: 350,740.00, Total Outstanding Dept ~ $295,600, FileNo#: 8374629, TS File#: 02-94773882 Trustee#: 02-i46oo4/9495822, Deed # 24/1993-488340

Section 404: Mechanics' Liens
Mira Mesa—Mark and Madge Webberson, reputed owner; Acme Roofing, Inc., claimant. Labor and material furnished at request of Mr. and Mrs. Mark Webberson at 5686 Winter Green Way
Amount Owing $7,696.00 (8405778)

Section 501: Notice of Petition
NOTICE OF PETITION TO ADMINISTER ESTATE OF Margaret I. Clark
CASE NUMBER P
To all heirs, beneficiaries, creditors, contingent creditors, and persons who may otherwise be interested in the will or estate of Margret I. Clark
A PETITION FOR PROBATE requests that Sonny A. Clark be appointed as personal representative to administer the estate of the decedent.

Technique #9: Visiting Sellers in Default in Person

Does this mean just show up on their doorsteps and knock on their doors? *Yes!* Let's face it. Out of the 50 other investors who could have the Notice of Default or lis pendens information about a seller in the early stages of foreclosure, 25 of them will mail a postcard or letter once in the mail to the sellers. Five will track down the owner's phone number and make a phone call. And only one or two will actually face their fears and knock on the sellers' doors.

This technique takes time and finesse to make it pay off for you. We'll walk you through what to say (and how to say it) when you arrive on the doorstep. But first, make sure it's worth your time for a personal visit. It's worthwhile when you reasonably expect there to be either a lot of equity in the house or the property is in an area where you want to acquire more long-term "keepers." If one or the other (ideally both) of these criteria is not met, then call or include the sellers in your mailing sequence, but don't waste your precious time visiting them.

You might be thinking that the homeowners wouldn't want you to come to their door. In many cases, they really are in desperate need of help. For example, Mike, a student in Columbus, Ohio, knocked on the door of a couple in the end stages of foreclosure. Mike agreed to make up the back payments and stop the foreclosure. His plan was to fix up the house, take over the payments, and resell it. There was a large chunk of equity in the house so Mike agreed to give 10 percent of his net profit back to the sellers to make it even more of a win-win.

What to Say When You Knock on the Seller's Door Cold

Here are two scripted variations of what to say when you're knocking on their doors and they don't expect you.

Script One: Works well if the seller is still in preforeclosure or if you're not quite ready to use gutsier Script Two.
Knock, knock . . . [Step back off the porch, turn sideways, assume a passive, harmless posture to put them at ease]
Owner: Yes?
Investor: Hi [*looking as harmless and* Bambi-like *as you can manage*] my name is Jim and I'm an investor who is looking to buy another house in this neighborhood and I was won-

dering if you knew of anyone in the area who might be at all open to selling their house if they got a fair offer on it.

Owner: Well, actually, I might want to sell my house.

Investor: Oh, OK, but I've probably caught you right in the middle of something, huh?

Owner: No, I was just making dinner. Now's as good a time as any.

And away you go—with the seller showing you the house and you following the Instant Offer System you'll learn in Chapter 5.

Script Two:
Knock, knock . . .

Owner: Yes, can I help you?

Investor: Hi, my name is Jim [*looking passive and harmless like a small puppy dog*] and I'm an investor who helps out folks who have a house that's in trouble. Is your house in trouble?

Owner: No, I don't know what you're talking about.

Investor: Oh . . . [*looking down at his clipboard and scratching his head*] I'm a little confused. It says here that the city thinks this house is behind in its payments. Heck, they even have it listed in the legal notice newspaper. But they probably got all that wrong, huh?

Owner: Can I see that paper?

Investor: Sure . . . [*Showing the owner the clipboard that has a listing of the owner's house with the date that the Notice of Default was filed or even a copy of the legal notice publication with the seller's property highlighted*]

Owner: [*A bit softer now*] Well, I guess I must be a bit behind. I thought the bank would work with me longer before they did this.

Investor: Yeah, I know . . . banks sure can play real tough with little fish like us. You know, though, a lot of times banks make mistakes when they send you all that paperwork, mistakes that can make them start all over again, from the beginning. I was visiting with another homeowner like yourself the other day when we spotted how the bank misspelled her name on the official notice. I helped her get another 60 days' delay in the process to give her more time to find her best solution. If you'd like, I'd be happy to take a quick look over the paperwork your bank sent you to see if I can spot any mistakes it made. Would you like me to sit down for a second and see if I can spot anything in the paperwork?

Owner: Would you!

And now you're in the house and connecting with the owner.

■ **David's Story**
I received an e-mail from a 34-year-old investor who found a great foreclosure deal by doing some research at the courthouse to find sellers in default. With the information he gleaned, he found the house and knocked on the door. The wife of the owner answered, welcomed him in, and, with her husband, visited for an hour and a half, and then worked out a sale arrangement. Our student funded the deal by taking on a money partner, splitting the $50,000 profit 50-50. The best part was that he helped the sellers avoid foreclosure.   ■

Technique #10: Real Estate Agents

Watch out for the trap of viewing real estate agents as your competition; nothing could be further from the truth. For the savvy investor, a good real estate agent is one of the best contacts to help find great foreclosure deals. Not only do agents have the ability and access to search the Multiple Listing Service (MLS, the proprietary database of homes listed for sale in a specific area), but they often have great networks of their own. This means many potential deals come across their radar screen first—so make sure you're the first investor they call!

How to Avoid the Five Biggest Mistakes When Working with a Realtor

Many investors searching for profitable deals waste a great amount of time by not knowing how to effectively work with real estate agents. We've boiled the common mistakes made down to five main ones and given you hints on how to sidestep them.

Mistake 1: Not clearly defining your buying criteria. Ask most real estate agents to find you a great deal and they'll ask you what you're looking for, what type of house, what price range, etc. What they usually won't ask you is what *you* consider a great deal! You don't want your real estate agent to simply give you a printout of all the listings in a specific area—that's a waste of time. Instead, narrow the field by giving your real estate agent specific criteria of what you expect from the properties she brings to you.

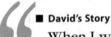
■ **David's Story**

When I work with agents where I buy properties, I give them my specific buying criteria. For example, I'll say I'm looking for condos, town houses, or single-family houses in the lower midprice range for the area. I also explain that I expect them to be able to tell me in two sentences or less *why* the seller is selling. Finally, I say the property must be priced at 80 percent or less of the "as is" value, or the seller must be flexible on the terms of the sale (such as open to a lease option, or subject to the existing financing, or a large owner-carry deal). I emphasize my need to make a profit by buying cheap, or to hold on to the property for a while, so the property needs to provide cash flow (i.e., produce enough rental income to cover all the holding costs). Using my criteria, they'll sift through the possible properties and bring me only ones that have a high likelihood of turning into a deal.   ■

Mistake 2: Relying on your agent to negotiate for you. Negotiations are too important for you to turn this responsibility over to another party. We feel even stronger—negotiations are not just your responsibilities, they are your opportunities. Besides, there is something inherently strange about a real estate agent negotiating for you. After all, the higher price you pay, the more money they make! (And this doesn't even take into consideration deals where your agent is representing both you AND the seller.) We strongly encourage you to master and keep control of the negotiations yourself.

Mistake 3: Accepting an agent's protests over the terms or price of your offer. We've heard it said that if you're negotiating a cash price and you're not embarrassed with how low your offer is, you're overpaying for the property. We take this one step further. If your agent is comfortable with your offer, that's the best indication you're not getting a good enough deal. Whatever you do, don't let your agent make your decisions about what to offer. *You* are the one who has to live with the deal you make, so be sure it's a great one. While an agent can be a great asset in helping you craft your offer, he will almost always want you to offer too much money or terms that are not quite good enough for you. So smile and reassure him that you value his input, and then go ahead and talk with the seller (with your agent) and put your offer in anyway. The worst the seller can say is no.

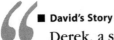

■ David's Story

Derek, a student from Tennessee, had been watching a house that had been sitting vacant for eight months. He looked up who owned the house, which ended up being a lender. After chasing down the right person to talk with, Derek discovered that the house had actually been listed on the MLS for months. When he asked the bank representative why the Realtor hadn't put up any signs or advertised the property, the bank rep didn't know.

So Derek called the listing agent, who told him the house was listed for $49,900. When Derek offered $23,800, the listing agent didn't look happy. A week later, he still hadn't heard back from the agent about his offer. When he called to follow up, the agent said Derek may have offended the bank. Derek was polite but firm and asked the agent to find out the status of his offer. Later that afternoon the agent called back. Both Derek *and* the agent were stunned—the bank had accepted his low cash offer. After he did $11,000 in repairs, the house was appraised for $74,000. Three months later, Derek sold it for $68,000 to a cash buyer. All totaled, Derek made $33,000 from an offer the agent thought had no chance of being accepted.   ■

Mistake 4: Discussing any critical information with the Realtor. It's been our experience that anything you tell your agent *will* get told to the other side, one way or another. Whether it is a stray comment he lets slip at the wrong time, or a tone of voice when he presents the offer, or a concession he wants to make when it really isn't in your best interest, somehow everything you tell your agent passes on to the other side. The only way to keep something that would weaken your negotiating position from the seller is to not tell your real estate agent.

■ Peter's Story

One of the biggest mistakes I see investors make is telling their Realtors the top amount they're willing to pay. Even if they go in with a lower price, invariably they come back saying the best they could do was right about the figure you gave them for your top price. It's just human nature. Of course, your Realtor wants the deal to work even more than you do. But this is a recipe for disaster. If I have an agent present an offer for me (which is rare because it's too important to rely on an agent to negotiate for me), I say that while I may be willing to go a tiny bit higher, my partner is really stuck on this number. I tell them to do the best they can and bring me the lowest number the seller will take just to make this deal work. I let them know that I'll approach my partner with this number and see if I can get him to go along with it, which is tough because my partner is really a hard case about this type of thing. You probably recognize the "good cop/bad cop" approach here, combined with an appeal to a higher authority. These tactics might be as old as time, but they still work magic and will make you a lot of money.   ■

Mistake 5: Working with agents who are struggling. You simply don't have the time to waste working with struggling agents. The top 10 percent of agents do more than 90 percent of the deals in most areas. So work with the best agents. This is especially important if you're buying lender-owned real estate or VA or HUD foreclosures. In these cases, ask around and find out who are the top three agents specializing in this niche. Interview all three and choose the best match for your needs and personality.

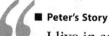

■ Peter's Story

I live in an area outside Denver called Genesee, a fairly pricey subdivision of 400 homes in the foothills of the Rockies. I have an excellent real estate agent whom I've developed a relationship with over the years. She knows that if she ever comes across a house in Genesee that's in foreclosure, I want to see about buying it. A while back, she called me up with information on a house that fit my criteria. Not only was the seller being foreclosed, but she was also in the final stages of a divorce. The house was listed at $372,000 and I put my offer in at $320,000. My offer was accepted. Today, three years later, that house is still rented to a tenant-buyer and is valued at more than $600,000.   ■

Technique #11: Networking with Attorneys

The "place of last resort" for many homeowners is in an office talking with an attorney. In fact, attorneys may know more sellers who own unwanted or problem properties than members of any other profession. While they can't pass out confidential client information, they can refer clients who need a fast sale or solution to call you. The best part of this is that you have an implied endorsement for these types of leads.

Following is a list of five different types of attorneys you can network with, along with the reason you might be a good fit for their clients:

1. *Probate.* Find people who just inherited a house they really don't want.
2. *Bankruptcy.* Find people who are in serious financial trouble and want to minimize the damage to their credit.
3. *Divorce.* Find people who need to liquidate assets quickly, or who were pushed into financial trouble because of the loss of their spouse's income or mounting legal fees.
4. *Real Estate.* Find people who are facing foreclosure and looking for a way out.
5. *Foreclosure specialist.* Specialize in processing foreclosures for lenders.

What can you do for these attorneys? Not only can you provide a valuable service to the attorneys' clients, but you can also refer more business to them. For example, during your time investing in foreclosures, you'll probably run into dozens of homeowners who will need legal advice about declaring bankruptcy and possibly about filing for that bankruptcy. Simply pass these referrals on to the bankruptcy attorney you're networking with. (We think you get the picture here.)

Technique #12: Send Out Your Bird Dogs

Bird dogs are people who spend a lot of their day outside, around houses, and are in places to spot bargain opportunities. The key is to tell them exactly what kinds of leads you are looking for. Tell them you are looking for:

- Vacant properties
- Ugly houses that need lots of work
- Sellers in financial trouble
- Houses where the utility company just turned off service because of nonpayment (notice posted on door)
- Homeowners who get lots of certified mail from lenders

Here is a list of potential bird dogs you can network with:

- Landscapers
- Utility repair people
- Meter readers (or other utility company employees)
- Postal delivery people
- FedEx drivers
- UPS drivers
- Airborne Express drivers
- Contractors
- Movers
- Newspaper delivery people

How much should you pay your bird dog as a finder's fee for a deal? While you'll have to decide for yourself, we've found that paying a bird dog a finder's fee between $250 and $1,000 cash for any deal he passes to you that you close on works well. The right number will depend on the value of properties in your area and the average profit per deal you realistically plan to make. For example, if you live in an area with $60,000 homes where you expect to net $15,000 to $30,000 per deal, you probably should pay $250 to $500 per deal a bird dog refers to you. If you live in an area with $500,000 homes where you expect to net $50,000 or more on your typical deal, then consider using $1,000 as your finder's fee. (Any more than $1,000 and it actually turns them off to finding more deals because it seems too good to be true.)

A student of ours in Arlington, Texas, had one of his bird dogs find him a couple in their mid-20s with a major gambling problem. The husband had lost the last two months' house payments, and it looked like they would lose the house, too. Tired of struggling to keep the house payments going, the sellers agreed to take $300 cash to walk away from it. Our student made up about $3,000 in back payments and bought the house subject to the sellers' financing. This was a cookie-cutter foreclosure deal that came from a neighborhood bird dog who received a finder's fee for his help.

Here's a script of exactly how to ask someone to help you find great deals. In this example, you open your front door and take delivery of a UPS package. As long as you're talking to the driver, why not ask him to help you find deals?

> *Investor:* Hi, thanks for bringing by that box.
> *UPS driver:* No problem, can I get your signature here.
> *Investor:* I'm Jason. What's your name?
> *UPS driver:* Scott.
> *Investor:* Scott, I'm an investor who buys houses in this area. You wouldn't by any chance know of any other drivers who ever come across a homeowner who needs to sell fast, or

who has a house that is run-down or vacant. The reason I ask is that sometimes I can buy these types of houses and pay the driver who passed the lead my way a healthy finder's fee—cash, of course.

UPS driver: Actually, I may be interested in that. What do I have to do?

Investor: You just call me, e-mail me, or leave me a note with the property address and, if you have it, the owner's name or phone number or any other contact information. I'll get to work on the deal and if I can put something together where I can profitably buy the house, I'll give you $500 cash the day I close on the house.

The biggest fear of a potential bird dog is that he'll pass you a lead, you'll follow up on it and buy the property, but won't pay him the finder's fee. When you know this up front, you understand that every bird dog will "test" you. They'll pass you a few leads to see what you'll do with them. If you want to pass this test with an A plus, make sure you not only follow up on the leads right away, but also follow up with your bird dogs to let them know what happened with their leads. Either e-mail them or leave them a phone message like the following:

David: Hi Scott, this is David. I just wanted to thank you for the two leads you passed my way three days ago. I also wanted to let you know what happened. The house on Briar Lane turned out not to be a fit; the seller owed way too much money on it. But the second lead for the Sunny Dale Road house looks promising. I talked with Jonathan, the owner, for about ten minutes yesterday and he is motivated to sell fast. I am meeting with him tomorrow to see the house and talk things over with him. I'll keep you posted on what happens with that one. Again, thanks for the referrals, and please keep them coming. I don't know if I'll be able to buy them all or any of them, but I do promise to keep you posted and any house I close on I'll pay you that $500 cash finder's fee on the day I close on the house. Bye . . .

Technique #13: Empower Your Friends and Family to Pass Leads Your Way

We've discovered that most investors can find at least one deal through the people they know in their personal network within six months of starting their investing. We tell Mentorship students that some acquaintance of theirs knows someone who has a house in trouble and needs to sell fast.

The biggest reason new investors don't ask people they know to help them find deals is fear—the fear that their friends and family will laugh at them or tear down their dreams. "After all," the new investor says, "my friends and family know I'm broke and was recently laid off. They'll never believe that I'm an investor." So here's a simple script to help you ask them for their assistance in finding deals, especially if you're afraid to tell them you are an investor.

Sample Script to Get Friends and Family to Find You Deals

> *Ring, ring . . .*
> *Friend:* Hello?
> *Investor:* Mark, hi, it's David [*say hello and catch up with each other for a bit . . .*]
> *Investor:* Mark, I wanted to ask a favor from you. I'm just getting started investing in real estate. I'm doing my best to do it the right way—I'm reading the books, listening to the home-study courses, taking the workshops, meeting with sellers, and putting offers out there. It's been a bit of a struggle to get

started. What I'm finding is that a lot of people are really negative about me getting started doing this and I wanted to ask if you'd be willing to give me a kind word from time to time when you see that I need it.

Friend: Of course, I'm willing to support you.

Investor: Thanks, Mark. Your encouragement really means a lot to me. Also, if you ever come across sellers who need to sell fast—maybe they're behind in their payments or they have a vacant property—would you be willing to let me know about it?

Friend: Sure, I would do that.

Investor: I knew I could count on your support, Mark. Look, I know that you would tell me about the house just to help me, but if I was in fact able to find a fit and buy the property, I'd like to send you and Sarah out to dinner on me. You pick the restaurant and I'll pick up the check. I'll even pop for a sitter for the kids too.

Friend: That sounds great!

See how easy it would be to approach your friends and family that way. You admit you're just getting started, that it's really hard going, and that you're simply asking for their support. It's almost an afterthought, albeit an important one, that you're asking them to help you find deals. Also, we've found that, with friends and family, offering to send them out to dinner is a great incentive and reward.

Technique #14: Buy Deals at Wholesale from Other Investors

You learned in Chapter 3 how you can sell your deals wholesale to other investors. But it works both ways. If you have the cash resources to close quickly—especially if you're willing to take on a rehab project—buying a deal from another investor is potentially a valuable lead source. Join your local real estate investor association and network with wholesalers in the group. Ask them to add you to their "buyers' list" so they'll contact you when they lock up a hot deal. For a cash fee, they will assign their contract with a seller over to you.

■ David's Story

Cheryl, one of our Mentorship program coaches, shared with me a deal she got for 60 cents on the dollar and paid a wholesaler $3,000 for his contract. She laughed when she told me he really wanted the names of her private lenders instead of the $3,000. Cheryl coyly smiled and gave him his money when she closed on the house.   ■

Technique #15: Network with Other Professionals

Think about all the people homeowners go to when they're in trouble. Then ask yourself how you can connect with these people and let them know you are an investor looking to buy more properties. Following is a list of professionals to consider:

- Doctors
- Chiropractors
- CPAs
- Insurance agents
- Paralegals
- Credit counselors
- Police officers
- Paramedics
- Religious leaders

With techniques 10 through 15, you've just learned about some giant sources to find profitable deals. If you read carefully through them, you'll notice 27 different referral sources.

Finding Foreclosure Deals Before Anyone Else Does

One problem with waiting for properties to show up on the radar screen of the Notice of Default or lis pendens lists or from other information source providers is that you're one of many investors getting the same lists at the same time. This can create competition.

Wouldn't it be powerful if you could get your hands on that list, or even the *precursor* to that list, ahead of possible competitors? Have we got your full attention now?

The following seven techniques do just that—find foreclosure deals *before* they appear on other investors' radar screens. It takes a good bit of legwork to tap into these seven techniques, but the payoffs can be huge. (Several of these ideas came from a brilliant investor named Joe Kaiser who developed a series of ideas to find underground sources to find foreclosure deals. You'll find more information about Joe and his ideas in "Your Bonus Web Pack" at the end of the book.)

Technique #16: "Trigger" Documents

What documents get recorded *before* a foreclosure is initiated? Here is a list of documents to tap into at your local courthouse or county recorder's office:

Notice of Appointment of Successor Trustee. If you live in a deed of trust state (you learned about this in Chapter 2), here's a powerful tip for you. Many lenders do not process their own foreclosures; they hire an outside firm to handle the entire foreclosure for them. To pass the legal power to this outside firm, the lender appoints this firm as the new Trustee under the deed of trust. This successor trustee will record the signed document from the lender called Notice of Appointment of Successor Trustee. Guess what?

You can look up any new appointments of successor trustees at your local recorder's office. Because lenders also appoint a new successor trustee if they sell the loan to another company—which commonly occurs—or for other reasons, you'll need to look for one more thing. Typically, there are a few companies in an area specializing in handling foreclosures for lenders. Search for these specific companies' names on the Notice of Appointment of Successor Trustee.

Filings for divorce. Foreclosures are often triggered by the ending of a marriage. The divorce process, like any other court process, begins with a specific filing at the local courthouse. In some areas, you can get access to this information; in other areas, you have to wait for these filed documents to age for 60 to 90 days; in still other areas, you won't ever be able to access them. However, it's worth trying to see what you can get at your local courthouse (or better yet, online through your local and county governments' Web sites).

Filings for bankruptcy. This legal process begins with a specific filing at your local courthouse. Investigate if you can get access to this information.

Probate filings. One of the most drawn-out legal processes is the probate process—the legal means by which a deceased person's will is "proven" and his or her property is disbursed. Because it's a public process, all of the deceased person's estate will be filed on record at the courthouse.

Technique #17: Research the Notice of Default List at the Courthouse

Because most other investors will wait to get the prepared list from their title company or local information source provider, you will get a two- to ten-day advantage over those waiting for their lists! Often this is the difference between being the only caller at the homeowner's door and being one of several investors competing for the same deal. Remember, only invest your time following up the juicy leads that have lots of equity.

Technique #18: Start a Foreclosure Service Business

While this one isn't appropriate for the beginning investor, if you're a seasoned investor, consider starting up a business helping lenders dealing with taking back distressed properties. Not only can you make a bit of profit from the service, but you can get insider access to leads on potential deals. The business would be involved in the following activities:

Process the foreclosure. For a flat fee, you can process the whole foreclosure yourself or work part-time for a company that processes foreclosures for lenders.

Recording foreclosure documents. You can run a service where you courier documents from lenders' offices or the local title company to the recorder's office where you record them for the lenders or local title company.

Weather-secure the house. If you live in a cold climate, consider working with lenders who have REO properties that need to be prepared for the winter cold.

Consult with sellers. You can create a service helping sellers in default work out forbearance agreements with their lenders. Those sellers who can't afford their properties can turn to you as an alternative to solve their problems. One student in Los Angeles uses only this single idea to find an average of four deals a month.

Technique #19: Go Through the Back Door

One strategy is to see if you can buy a bad debt that is secured by a piece of real estate. Not only can you buy this debt for pennies on the dollar, but you can start the foreclosure yourself to get the property. Once you've acquired the debt (or even better, the option to buy the debt at a huge discount), you can call up the homeowner and negotiate a great buy on the property.

Here's a list of the types of debt to look for:

- Distressed notes (i.e., promissory notes secured by a property)
- Mechanics' liens (e.g., a contractor who replaced a roof but was never paid for the work)
- Judgments that have attached to the property (e.g., a judgment from a car accident where the winner of the judgment was never paid)

Technique #20: Establish Relationships with Lenders in the REO or Loss Mitigation Department

Remember, the REO department is the place where the "real estate owned" by the lender is handled. Banks don't want property; they want to get rid of the properties and get the money recirculated into new loans. You can get the inside edge in some sweet deals if you have a solid relationship with the people who handle this for the bank. Also, the loss mitigation department—the part of the bank where bad loans end up—can be a great referral source if you carefully build relationships there.

Technique #21: Establish Relationships with Realtors Who Specialize in REO Properties

In many areas, a few real estate agents specialize in selling *all* the REO properties for local lenders. These agents have taken the time to build the relationships with lenders and the track records to gain their trust. You can tap into this network by working with these Realtors to buy REO properties.

Technique #22: Create Your Own Ugly- or Vacant-House List

As you can imagine, one of the first signs of a pending foreclosure is that homeowners stop spending time and energy taking care of the yard. So drive through the areas you want to buy properties in and write down the addresses of any houses you see that look vacant or where the yard has been let go. After all, some homeowners facing foreclosure figure they no longer have a vested interest, so why should they pay to water the lawn? Additionally, get your bird dogs or others in your network to refer these types of leads to you.

Here are five ways to find owners of vacant houses:

1. Knock on the door. You never know—they might just be home. If they're not home, leave a letter or note on their door telling them you're a local investor who might want to buy their house and to please call you.
2. Visit the neighbors and let them know you're an investor who's interested in buying that eyesore on their street and fixing it up to be a positive addition to their neighborhood.
3. Mail a letter first-class, clearly marked, "Do not forward—address correction service requested." If there's a forwarding address, the U.S. Post Office will send you notice of what the updated address is.

4. Look up who owns the house and their mailing address in the tax mailing address records (online or at the recorder's office or through a local title company). From this, try to get a phone number from the telephone information service in the city where the owners live. Or mail a handwritten note to the owners and include them in your mailing sequence (described earlier in this chapter).

5. Search on the Web. (Note: As part of Your Web Bonus Pack at the back of the book, you'll find links to specific Web sites you can use to track down owners of abandoned properties.)

The real key is to get out and mix with people who can lead to deals. Try out a variety of the different ideas you've learned here and find three to five that work well in your area. Keep doing these successful things over and over. Don't look for your marketing to be exciting; look for it to make you money. Sadly, we've watched too many investors change a successful marketing campaign because the investor got bored with the "same old same old."

Tracking Your Marketing Efforts

So how will you know what works? By tracking your marketing efforts in these three ways:

1. Measure the cost of the campaign. This means measuring and recording the time, energy, and money you invested in a particular marketing campaign. Remember, it's not just the monetary cost of the ads or letters; it's also the time it took from you and the effort it took to get the work done. Look at the *real* cost.

2. Measure the response of the campaign. This is best done by having all calls from a specific lead source go to a separate voice-mail or extension for your voice-mail system. For information on the system we've been using for several years, visit the American Real Estate Investors Association Web site at <www.americanreia .com>. This association offers an inexpensive preprogrammed system for all its members. Also make sure you double-check this type of tracking by systematically asking all sellers who responded to a specific marketing campaign how they first heard about you. If the two answers conflict, usually your voice-mail tracking is more reliable than the seller's memory. Still, it's useful to have the backup information from asking the sellers where they heard about you. Also take a moment to ask these sellers what part of your marketing campaign or message motivated them to respond.

3. Match up the real costs and the responses with your bottom-line successes. How many deals did you sign up? How many of these deals were keepers that made you money? You're not measuring your marketing activities by the number of leads but, rather, by the number of dollars those leads help you earn and the effort required to earn those dollars.

You can find great foreclosure deals. They are out in your marketplace. And the homeowners of these properties are in dire need of your help. You win by making a profit and they win by solving a pressing problem.

So what are you waiting for? Put down this book and put these ideas to work at making you money!

The Instant Offer System—Five Simple Steps to "Yes"

Imagine you've worked hard to find sellers in default who sound motivated over the phone. You've passed through your initial phone qualification and the financial details all look good.

You've spent a total of four hours finding this one seller and setting up an appointment to meet at the house to talk about buying it. You feel a bit nervous, but you put that aside and focus on the excitement of potentially signing up your first, or next, deal.

Fast-forward to your arrival at the seller's house. You pull up and park on the street in front of the house. You get your first real look at the house from the street and think it looks just like a normal house. No one would ever be able to tell by looking at the house from the curb that the seller is five payments behind and on the verge of losing it.

You step out of your car and walk up to the front door. At this point, all the "cool" you felt anticipating this meeting disappears. Your heart is racing like a runaway stallion. It's all you can do to keep yourself from turning around, getting back in your car, and driving away.

"What am I going to say to the seller? What are my first words exactly? What questions should I ask? In what order? How should I say them? How will I know what to offer the seller?"

Have we got your attention now?

We're about to give you the road map—your step-by-step guide—to the answers to all these questions and more. You'll learn exactly how to handle a meeting with a seller in default—every time.

Those who have read our books or purchased one of our advanced home-study courses have already learned about the negotiating strategies and techniques we teach. At the heart of these negotiating techniques is the five-step process we've developed and refined over the past eight years. We call it the "Instant Offer System" or "IOS" for short.

The Big Picture of the Instant Offer System

What comes next is a distillation of our best negotiating secrets as they directly apply to buying foreclosures. When you finish working with this section, you'll know what to say and in what order so you have the best chance to close the deal.

The IOS is made up of five distinct steps that must happen in the correct order to get the seller emotionally and intellectually ready to sign the deal on the spot. The words *on the spot* tell it all. You'll always have the best chances to put a deal together if you get it signed up at your first meeting with the seller. To do this, spend the time talking with the seller and helping him or her emotionally and intellectually process what you're offering.

Here are the five steps:

1. Connect with the seller.
2. Set up an "up-front agreement."
3. Build the seller's motivation.
4. Talk about the money.
5. Take the "what if" step.

Five Steps to Get Sellers in Foreclosure to Say "Yes"

Let's go through each of these steps in detail so that when you're finished reading (and rereading) this section, you'll have all the tools you need to go out and negotiate a moneymaking deal on your own.

Step One: Connect with the Seller

Start by building rapport with the seller. Imagine you were a seller and you were in a financially vulnerable position. How would you feel about some "investor" coming over to talk about buying your house?

Can you imagine how cautious and guarded you'd be? How closed emotionally you might be? Your job is to take the first five to ten minutes to establish a connection and affinity with the sellers.

How do you do that? You gently ask the sellers questions about themselves and their lives, building bridges wherever you genuinely can. The fact is, people like people who are just like them. So as you go through Step One, you'll draw sellers out of their shells and get them to talk candidly. Wherever possible, you'll highlight when you're just like they are.

Here's an example of how this conversation might go. Imagine you, the investor, are walking through the house with the seller showing you around.

> *Investor:* Are these your kids? [*You point to the photo on the end table*]
> *Samantha:* Yes, they are. That's Mark, my oldest, Sylvia, and Jonathon.
> *Investor:* How old are they now?
> *Samantha:* Mark's 26, Sylvia's 16, and Jonathon is 12.

Investor: My kids are 12 and 14 [*building a bridge*]. So does it get any easier when they hit their 20s? [*smiling*]

Samantha: It sure does. You know, I always thought it was real important to remember that we were all teenagers once and we survived it. Although looking back, I'm not sure how my parents survived my teen years. [*Notice how the seller is loosening up a bit.*]

Investor: I know exactly what you mean. I think I was probably the toughest of the bunch for my parents to raise. [*Building a bridge*] What's your oldest doing now?

Samantha: He's married with a child on the way. He lives in Seattle and works for a financial company out there.

Investor: Wow, you're going to have a grandchild! That must be so exciting for you. How much longer until the due date . . .

You get the idea; the first step of the IOS is to make a friend.

We know some people will complain that they can't build rapport with the seller because they feel awkward and don't know what to ask. So here's a list of surefire questions to ask sellers. They will jump-start the conversation if you ever feel stuck.

- Where did you grow up?
- Do you have any kids?
- How old are they?
- What do you do for a living?
- How did you get started in that career?
- What do you like to do for fun?

How to Avoid the Two Biggest Mistakes When Building Rapport

Mistake 1: Spending too much time on rapport (and not moving to Step Two fast enough). At some point, a beginning investor finds himself wasting hours of his time making friends with a seller who just isn't in a position to sell the investor her house. The investor spends so much time building rapport that by the time he determines that the property obviously isn't a fit, the investor has wasted several hours of his precious time.

What do you really think causes an investor to remain in Step One of the IOS and not move on? If you said *fear,* you're right. The ideal amount of time to spend building rapport during Step One is five to ten minutes.

Mistake 2: Thinking that Step One of the IOS is done just once, ticked off, and forgotten. Building rapport with the seller is something you'll have to do throughout your meeting with the seller. While you should spend only five to ten minutes before moving on to Step Two (setting an up-front agreement), that doesn't mean you're finished building rapport.

Throughout your negotiation, you will have to gauge your connection with the seller and look for opportunities to broaden and deepen this connection. But you have to balance this need to maintain the connection with your equally important need to move the conversation forward.

Step Two: Set an Up-front Agreement

What is your most precious resource as an investor? Some people will say money. Others will say good credit. We say it's time. Yet we watch so many beginning investors work for *free!* By this, we mean they invest all kinds of time and energy before they have a definite commitment from the seller that they have reached an agreement.

We're not willing to work for free and we don't think you should either. Instead, make it understood up front that you'll spend the time it takes to work through the situation and the details, provided the seller agrees early in the conversation that when it's over, both of you will let each other know exactly where you stand—either you have a fit or you don't. Period. That simple.

In its plainest terms, an up-front agreement is simply a commitment from you and the seller to say *yes* or *no* at the end of your conversation about the property.

Here's how it sounds:

> *Investor:* Samantha, I'm willing to sit and invest the time to listen to all the details of your situation and to talk through all the possible options we can come up with. All I ask is that when we're done talking this through, if what we talk through obviously isn't a fit for you, that you be willing to let me know. If it just isn't a fit, are you willing to tell me that?
>
> *Samantha:* Sure.
>
> *Investor:* I appreciate that. I'm letting you know that you're not going to hurt my feelings. On the other hand, if what we talk through *is* a fit for you, are you willing to let me know that when we're done here today?
>
> *Samantha:* Yes, if it's a fit, I can tell you that.
>
> *Investor:* Now I'll be doing the same thing in reverse. If I can't see a way where I can meet your needs and make a profit for myself, then I'm not going to want to buy your house. Are you OK if I have to tell you no, I don't want to buy it? I mean, it wouldn't be anything personal about you; it would just be me saying it's not a fit.
>
> *Samantha:* I understand this has to work for both of us.
>
> *Investor:* Exactly, and if I feel it's a fit, then I'll let you know that too. I'll say, "Samantha, this is a fit for me too." So

what we're agreeing to do up front is to let each other know when we're done exactly where we stand. Either *no, it's absolutely not a fit.* Or *yes, it is a fit.* Is that what we just agreed to do? [*This is called "reinforcing" the up-front agreement.*]
    Samantha: Yes it is . . . [*and on to the next step*].

Do you see how powerful that language and strategy is? It's your way of telling sellers that you'll put your time in to see if it's a fit, *if and only if* they'll promise to give you a decision right at the end.

■ **Peter's Story**
There is going to come a time when you're scared to firmly set an up-front agreement. When that moment comes, remember that I coached you to do it anyway. Oh, you'll think the language will sound stilted and strange, but do it anyway. Then, in the closing moves of your negotiation, if you need to, gently but firmly remind the seller of your mutual commitment up front to make a decision. You'll find this clear stance helps liberate you from wondering what's going to happen next. Honor this agreement and hold the seller to it too.   ■

Step Three: Build the Seller's Motivation

At this point you've set the stage to really begin your negotiation. You've connected with the seller, built rapport, and set your up-front agreement (by which the seller has agreed to give you a decision at the end of your negotiation).

Now it's time to move to the next step, which is negotiating with the seller on an emotional level. In this step, you help the seller connect with all the pressing reasons why she needs to sell and why you are her best option. We call this "building the seller's motivation."

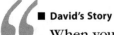

■ David's Story

When you want to build a seller's motivation, think about how great athletes perform. They first carefully warm up and stretch before they go out and compete. They know that if they start without this preparation, they might pull a muscle or otherwise injure themselves. It's the same with sellers. You need to help them warm up to the idea of selling to you at a price and terms that allow you to make a conservative profit. In the motivation step, you're helping them stretch and warm up to find a fit for both of you.   ■

A key outcome to be reached in Step Three of the IOS is to help sellers break out of the denial they may be living in. So many sellers who are in foreclosure have deluded themselves into believing that it's not really happening. They rationalize away their situation or, even worse, block it out completely. Unless you are able to help them work through any barriers and be emotionally present with the consequences they might face from their situation, you'll be hard-pressed to both help the seller and get a great buy on the property.

One of the things we covered in *Making Big Money Investing in Real Estate* was something called "negative phrasing." This one idea will turn upside down many of the traditional notions of negotiating with a seller.

When sellers are in foreclosure, they are scared some investor will come in and steal their house. And when people are motivated by fear, they look for what is wrong, because they feel that if they can spot what's wrong, they can protect themselves. A seller who is motivated by fear will "mismatch," meaning he'll look for what's wrong. This is a term from Neuro-Linguistic Programming (NLP) that refers to a person's tendency to see and say the opposite of what he's told. For example, if you say to the seller that he'll never get the price he wants, he'll be even more convinced that he will. If you say that the condition of the house isn't good, he'll argue that it is good.

This is a leverage point for you in negotiations. *Whenever you can accurately predict how the other person in a negotiation will behave, you can use this information to be more effective.*

Here are a few simple examples of how to use negative phrasing to build the seller's motivation:

Example one:

Investor: You mentioned that you thought about just refinancing as a way out. The mortgage brokers you talked with probably have already got that process going, right?

Seller: Well, actually, the guy I talked with said with my credit, I wouldn't be able to refinance the house.

Example two:

Investor: How else have you tried to sell the house?

Seller: We've been selling it "for sale by owner" for the last few weeks.

Investor: And that's been working really well for you?

Seller: Actually, it hasn't been working at all.

Example three:

Investor: You told me on the phone that you met yesterday with another investor. How did that go? I mean you probably really connected with him, huh?

Seller: Not really, he was a bit rude and pushy and I ended up asking him to leave.

Do you get the idea? Rather than coming out and saying what you mean directly, you simply say the opposite and let the seller step into the powerful role of the one getting to correct you. This is one important reason that negative phrasing works so well when negotiating with sellers in default. Considering how powerless many sellers in their situations feel, you can probably see how by giving them the emotional currency of feeling powerful you can really draw them out of their shell and connect emotionally with them. Also notice how you are getting the seller to be the one who argues for your case, that she really is in trouble and does need your help. After all, who is the seller more likely to believe, herself or you?

Remember, sellers who are in foreclosure are embarrassed to admit, even to themselves, what their situation is, so they live in denial. That is why it's so important to spend the time with them to build their motivation. We mentioned that Step One (connecting with the seller) of the IOS should take five to ten minutes, Step Three (building motivation) should take you closer to 30 minutes—the longer the better.

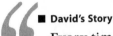

■ David's Story

Every time I watch Peter negotiate on a property, I am still awed. Over the years, I've modeled his incredible ability to help sellers get in touch with the real reasons they need to sell fast. He's just so good at it. That's one of the reasons why our IOS of today is vastly better than it was eight years ago—because I've modeled all the powerful improvements Peter has come up with over the years. Imagine for a moment what it would be like to go out on appointment after appointment with him as your coach and mentor. When people ask me how I got to be so good at negotiating and investing, I explain how Peter made me his first Mentorship student and helped me make my first million by age 31, starting out with no knowledge of real estate at all.   ■

Here's a sample of a transcript of an actual negotiation:

Investor: So, Samantha, you were telling me on the phone a few days ago that you had just received a letter from your lender saying it was about to start the official foreclosure. A lot of people would be scared by that kind of letter, but you probably just took that in stride, right? [*Negative phrasing*]

Samantha: Not really; it freaked me out. I mean it was really scary to get that letter.

Investor: Oh, really . . . tell me more about what you felt when you got that letter . . . [*Voice dropping lower in tone and softer in volume*]

Samantha: I remember thinking to myself, What am I going to tell my family about this if I lost the house?

Investor: I imagine that must have been hard for you to think about. I know a lot of people would just run away and hide from the truth. Heck, you were probably tempted to just run away from what that letter meant. [*Negative phrasing*]

Samantha: No, I knew I couldn't run away. I mean, sure I thought about it for a moment, I still do at times, but I know that isn't going to help any.

Investor: Well, if worst came to worst and you lost the house to the bank, I'm sure your family would be supportive and wouldn't judge you in any way. [*Negative phrasing said with big eyes*]

Samantha: They'd be there for me, but they sure would let me know how I had messed up.

Investor: How do you mean? [*Scrunchy face, voice getting softer*]

Samantha: They'd make comments and whatnot. It wouldn't be too obvious, but they would take little shots and stuff like that. I don't want to have to deal with that when I'm back visiting for the next 10 or 20 years . . .

And the conversation would continue on along those lines. Go back and read through the sample transcript one more time. This time, look for other techniques used in this negotiation to help the seller emotionally associate closely with her situation instead of holding it at a distance. (Hint: We did this when we asked questions like, "Tell me, what did you feel when you got that letter?" and, "How do you mean?")

You're giving the seller prompts so she goes into more detail about how she feels. This scares a lot of investors. They say, "I wanted to buy foreclosures because I like houses, or because I like running numbers, not to have some kind of touchy-feely conversation with a seller." The truth is that "houses and numbers" are not the business you're in. *Connecting emotionally with sellers who need your help is your core business.* Never forget this.

One of the greatest skills you can develop is your capacity to be comfortable guiding other people through tough emotional experiences.

Step Four: Talk about the Money

Now you are ready to talk through the numbers with the seller. Notice that you needed to save this part of the negotiation for near the end. One of the biggest mistakes we see investors make is to negotiate the numbers—the money—without building the seller's motivation first. This can cost you tens of thousands of dollars on every deal.

■ **Peter's Story**

Class after class, our Mentorship students find that the Purchase Option Money Game they play at our three-day Intensive Training is the most powerful part of the training. Not only do they get to role-play the whole IOS, but they have defined criteria to help them make sure they stay on track. One of the most important ways they keep from getting penalty points (and are more likely to be able to "keep" their deals) is to always cover motivation before money. Remember this the next time you negotiate on a house. No matter how temptingly the seller brings up the subject of money early in the negotiation, keep firm and fully cover the seller's motivation before you move on to discuss money. You'll always get a much better deal this way.   ■

There are two goals for the Money Step. First, to get all the seller's financial details on the table. Second, to gather all this information and *at the same time, lower the seller's expectations* about the amount of money she'll receive and when she'll receive it.

You might be thinking that you could never do both of these things. But we believe that anyone, with a little coaching, can become a great negotiator. Great negotiators are made, not born.

Are you open to our coaching? We are about to give you the word-for-word language patterns that can lead to a slam dunk when negotiating with sellers in default. Still, it's up to you to put them into practice.

> ***Insider Secret:*** Learning to negotiate well is like learning a foreign language. The best way is to have plenty of repetition and immerse yourself in the sounds of native speakers. (That's why we recommend to students who get our home-study course to listen to the negotiating sections over and over again.) At a certain point, you'll find yourself able to use just the right language, at the right moment, in the right way. It's similar to how you take in and learn lyrics to songs. After hearing the song over and over, one day you just know the words. It's effortless.

The best way to learn how to negotiate money is to listen in to an actual negotiation like this one:

> *Investor:* So what do you think the house is conservatively worth, Samantha?
>
> *Samantha:* About $350,000.
>
> *Investor:* Oh, it's worth conservatively $330,000 to $350,000, OK . . . [*Range technique—see our book* Making Big Money Investing in Real Estate *for this and 22 other powerhouse negotiating techniques*]
>
> *Samantha:* Actually, I think it's worth $350,000.

Investor: Oh, pardon me . . . $340,000 to $350,000.

Samantha: Yeah, I guess it's around there.

Investor: Let me ask you, What did you realistically think you would get, considering the house's situation?

Samantha: I thought I'd get at least $335,000 or more.

Investor: Oh, OK . . . you thought you'd get $320,000 to $335,000 . . . [*If the range technique works once, use it again!*] Let's see . . . a thought just occurred to me, if a real estate agent came to you and said he could get the house sold in the next 30 days, and you were convinced he could get it sold for you in the next 30 days for, let's say, the full $320,000 or maybe even a little bit more, you'd probably turn that offer down, huh? [*Negative phrasing*] Or maybe you wouldn't? You tell me . . .

Samantha: At this point, I'd probably just take it to be done with all this mess.

Investor: That makes sense. Let's see, 6 percent of $320,000 is . . . 6 percent of 100,000 is $6,000, so we times that by three to get . . . $18,000, plus 6 percent of the $20,000 is about . . . what, $1,200. So I'm getting the full commission as roughly $20,000; is that what you're getting?

Samantha: Yes, I'd get about $300,000 after all is said and done.

Investor: I think you're right. You'd walk away with the $300,000, less your share of the closing costs [*notice how you just slipped that one back into the conversation*]. What do you think the closing costs would be, Samantha? I had a real estate agent friend who told me that the costs usually are about 1 percent, so in this case that would be what, around $3,000 or so. Does that sound like about what you thought they would be?

Samantha: I hadn't really thought to add them in. But I guess you're right. Gosh, it doesn't really seem like I'd get much of anything.

(Note: You haven't written any number down until you get to this bottom number of $297,000, which you write down and label as "full price amount to seller." Remember, in any negotiation, the person who is the one to label different pieces of information has a tremendous advantage in that negotiation.)

Investor: What was it you owe against the property?

Samantha: $280,000.

Investor: Is that all on one first mortgage or spread between two or more loans?

Samantha: No, that's all on one first mortgage.

Investor: And the payment on that is . . .

Samantha: $2,350, and that includes the taxes and insurance.

Investor: And how many months is the house behind right now? [*Notice you said "the house," not "the seller."*]

Samantha: I'm four payments behind, going on five in two more weeks when the next payment is due.

Investor: Oh, so the house is about $10,000 behind as of the next payment, plus late fees and any other fees your lender tacks on . . .

STOP! You are done with Step Four of the IOS. You've gotten all the financial details down on paper in a way that has lowered the seller's expectation of what she will get.

Now it's time to move on to Step Five—the "what if" step.

Step Five: Take the "What If" Step

What if there was a powerful two-word phrase that would *guarantee* you'd never be rejected by a seller ever again? We're not saying it's possible, but again, what if it were possible that these two words would mean a seller would never reject any formal offer you made? If you could have these two words, what would it mean to you? How valuable would these words be to you in your investing? Would you be willing to donate $1,000 to your favorite charity just to get an e-mail from us telling you what these two words were and exactly how to use them? You would? OK, we're a little confused here. Why would these words even be so important to you?

All kidding aside, we hope you just noticed the language pattern of the preceding paragraph because it parallels exactly the tack you will take with the seller in this final step of the IOS.

The two words that guarantee you'll never have a seller reject any formal offer you make are *what if.* These are the two most powerful words in any negotiation because they commit you to nothing, but commit the other person to everything.

You can use these words effectively by qualifying any offer you choose to make to the seller with these two words. Then, before you "make" the offer, that person tells you that she would accept it. It's so simple yet powerful that many would-be investors forget to use them when negotiating with a seller in foreclosure.

Here's a transcript of how those words might sound in action. We'll be building on our negotiation with Samantha. At its completion, we'll highlight several of the powerful techniques used in this transcript that you can immediately put to work to make your negotiations with any seller in foreclosure more profitable.

> *Investor:* Samantha, here's an idea, you'll probably hate it [*negative phrasing*], but what if I were to make up the back payments and buy the property, and just take over the payments from here on out? I'm not sure if I'd be willing to do this or not just yet [*reluctant buyer*], but what if I were able to talk my partner [*higher authority*] into doing this? Is that something we should even talk about, or probably not? [*Negative phrasing*]

> *Samantha:* No, I don't hate it. We should definitely talk about it.

Investor: Oh, OK . . . I'm a little confused here, I guess it's been a long day or something. What about me making up your back payments and buying the property, and then taking over your payments each month from here on out—would that even work for you? [*Scrunchy face*]

Samantha: Well, you'd stop the foreclosure so I wouldn't have that on my credit record for the next seven years.

Investor: Why's that even important to you?

Samantha: Because my credit is important to me. I mean, it affects my buying another house someday. It affects my car insurance costs. Besides, I just don't want to be the type of person who doesn't honor her obligations.

Investor: Oh, so if I'm hearing you right, you want me to make up your back payments, buy the property, and take over making the monthly payments from here on out [*giving the seller full credit for the idea*]. Did I get that right?

Samantha: Yes, that's what I want you to do.

By the way, if you liked the negotiating techniques you've learned about so far, make sure you get a copy of *Making Big Money Investing in Real Estate* right away. We went to great lengths to build on the 23 negotiating techniques taught in that book. We know, you're thinking that you just spent $20 on this book; now these authors tell me to get their *other* book. Yes, that's exactly what we're saying. When you get it and read it cover to cover within 30 days of buying it, if you don't feel it's worth ten times the price, we'll refund every penny you spent on it. This isn't the publisher talking; it's Peter and David's guarantee.

It's that good. If you don't agree, send a quick note with your store receipt and the book. Tell us you want a refund and we'll send it, no questions asked. (See our contact information at the end of this book.) Do we have a deal? Heck, you probably hate that idea. [*Negative phrasing*]

How to Avoid the Seven Biggest Negotiating Mistakes Most Investors Make

#1. Chasing the Deal

The best negotiators know that they can't appear to be too anxious to make a deal. In the negotiating game, to be as effective as you want, you need to be a bit coy. Remember, reluctant buyers never chase after the deal; they seem hesitant, almost as if they are ready to walk away from the deal at any moment. This reluctance fuels the seller's desire to want the deal even more.

Here are two quick examples of how reluctant buyers sound and the specific language patterns they use:

Example one:
Seller: What do you think you are willing to pay me for the house?

Investor: Well, Mr. Seller, to be frank, I'm still not sure I even want the house. What with all the craziness that is going on in the world today, I'm just not sure now is the time to pick up another investment property. May I ask you a few more questions to see if I even want to buy the house? [*Imagine you were the seller and heard such reluctant language. Can't you just feel your stomach sink?*]

Example two:
Investor: I'm not sure if I could even do this, but what if I was able to negotiate with your lender to have it accept a lot less money as full payment on what you owe? If I could do that, and I'm not sure I could, but if I could, would that be a fit for you, or probably not?

Seller: Yes, that would be a fit. Can you really do that?

Investor: Well, I'm not really sure I can, but I'll give it my best go. If I could, that would mean you could just walk away and start fresh somewhere else . . .

Do you see the patterns of qualifying everything added into the negative phrasing? They work powerfully when combined like this.

#2. Selling the Seller on the Deal

Remember, when you are negotiating with a seller you need to play the role of the reluctant buyer. So often we see other investors forget what they are doing and try to sell the seller on the deal. Here's what this sounds like:

Average investor: Mr. Seller, what if I were able to buy your house for all cash at closing? This would give you immediate debt relief [*benefit one*], which would mean no more angry bank letters in the mail or bank bill collectors calling you up on the phone [*more benefits*]. Can you imagine how good that would feel to be free of this property?

You might be asking what's wrong with this example. After all, "benefits sell" so why shouldn't you stack benefit on top of benefit to make your solution to the seller's problem even more appealing. All we can say is that it just isn't effective to sell the seller on the deal. And this is especially true when the seller is feeling vulnerable like he surely must feel if he is in foreclosure. Here's what we anticipate would happen (the seller's response) in this example:

Seller: Well, I don't know. It all sounds good but somehow it just sounds too easy. Besides, you'd never pay me enough to be something I'd accept. [*See how the seller is getting a bit nervous here.*]

Average investor: I understand how you feel, Mr. Seller, but consider what it would really mean to you if we could get you the cash you need to just cut your ties to the house and get on with your life. We're talking all cash at closing. You do like the sound of all cash at closing, don't you?

Seller: Of course, I like the sound of all cash, but it's just not going to work for me the way you describe it. I appreciate your time, but I just don't think we'll find a fit here.

And the more the average investor pushes the seller, the firmer the seller's stance becomes that there just isn't a fit. What the average investor didn't realize is that in *every* negotiation there is always an eager party who wants the deal to close, and a reluctant party who cares significantly less if the deal closes. The average investor mistakenly chose the wrong role!

Then the average investor compounded the error by trying to "convince" the seller. We've found that you can't convince motivated sellers of anything, you can only help lead them to the conclusions you want them to reach.

If we were negotiating this deal, we would use the following language to move the seller to the same conclusions that the average investor tried to jam down his throat.

Investor: Mr. Seller, if I did decide to buy this house, which I'm not sure I want to yet, I probably would want to do it with an all-cash offer. But you probably want an offer where you don't get all cash at closing but rather get paid payments over time, huh?

Seller: Actually, I prefer getting all cash at closing.

Investor: Really? Why would you want all cash at closing even though you know it will mean you get less for the house because any investor would need to make a fair profit for even wanting to buy the place?

Seller: Because it would get me out from under all this debt and let me get a clean break.

Investor: What about getting out from under the debt and getting a clean break is even important to you?

Seller: You don't know what it's been like for me and my family, what with all the nasty letters from the bank, and the stress of not knowing what to do. I just want to be done with it, to cut my ties and get myself and my family a clean break from this house.

Do you see how a little more subtle approach was so much more effective because it harnessed the seller's natural tendency to be much more comfortable with the conclusions he makes compared to the facts and "benefits" you spoon-fed him to force him to agree to your conclusions?

Look for this *big* danger point when closing on the deal: Remember that during the "what if "step, the investor asks the seller if that solution was something he should even talk about? When sellers say yes, most investors *blow it.* "How?" you ask. By getting all excited with the seller's provisional yes and rushing into the opening with as many benefits as the investor can fit in, as quickly as he can. ("Oh great, Mr. Seller, this will really take the strain off you and your family and give you back your peace of mind. I bet that peace of mind is worth everything to you, huh?")

Mistake! Instead of rushing in like that, which only makes the seller put up his guard and start to look for what's wrong (What's wrong with this picture? I wonder what I'm I missing that makes this investor seem so eager here?), use a little negotiating leverage to get the seller to close the deal himself!

Here's exactly how to do this:

Investor: What if I were to make up your back payments and buy the house? Then I'd take over your payments every month. I'm not sure at this point I'm even willing to do this, but what if I was willing to? Is that something we should even talk about, or you probably hate the idea, huh?

Seller: No, I don't hate the idea.

Investor: Oh, OK . . . What about me making up your back payments and taking over your payments is even a fit for you?

Do you see how you are getting the seller to follow up with the benefits he gets if he does business with you? The seller is literally *selling himself* on the benefits. And, of course, this is a thousand times more powerful than any benefits you could convince him of.

Tap into human nature in your negotiations to become even better at closing deals. Let the seller sell himself and you on the deal. Don't ram benefits down the seller's throat; instead, let him tell you all the reasons he thinks make your offer the right fit.

#3: Being the Ultimate Decision Maker

One important rule is: Make sure the other side always has all their decision makers with them while you always have a "higher authority" to appeal to elsewhere. This higher authority could be a partner or board of directors or spouse or attorney. While it might seem effective to be the one in charge—the decision maker—nothing could be further from the truth. Every investor needs a higher authority in all negotiations.

By using a higher authority you are creating an environment where you can accept concessions from the seller but can't make certain concessions yourself. Or if you make these critical concessions, you get to qualify them with your need to get them past your partner, a higher authority. Also, this helps you maintain the position of the reluctant buyer who needs to be sold on buying the property.

Here is what this sounds like in a negotiation:

Investor: So if I'm hearing you right, you want us to get you $8,000 cash, plus make up your back payments and take over the monthly payments from here on out. Did I get that right?

Seller: Yes.

Investor: Are you sure that would even work for you? I mean, before I try to get my partner to go for this I want to make certain that you are sure it is a total fit for you.

Seller: Yes, it's a fit for me.

Investor: And why was it again that you felt that this was a real fit?

Seller: Like I mentioned before, it gives me enough money to start fresh and to keep my credit intact.

Did you see how the use of the partner (*higher authority*) allowed you to get the seller to make a much firmer commitment that the deal works for her?

#4. Taking Credit for the Solution

A pattern we've seen play out frequently is when one party receives the financial payoff while the other party gets the emotional payoff of being important and smart. We've also noticed that rarely will one person receive both payoffs. So what will it be for you? Are you willing to give the seller the emotional and psychological payoff in order to make a healthy profit? Glad to hear it!

One of the most important ways to give sellers emotional currency is to give them 100 percent credit for the "solution" they come up with. Don't let your ego step in and claim ownership of the fancy solution *you* dreamed up. Be generous, making sure you compliment the sellers on their creative ideas.

Here is what this sounds like in a real negotiation:

Investor: Let's see, when you added up all those estimated repairs we went through, what was the final amount you came up with?

Seller: $35,000.

Investor: OK, so let's see . . . the price you said you would take just to be done with the house, and which you felt the house would get if it were fixed up, was $340,000. Did I get that straight?

Seller: Yes, you have that right.

Investor: So let's see, after we factor in the repairs of $35,000 to get the house right to sell fast for the $340,000, and after we factor in the $5,000 in back payments, and the $270,000 that the bank is owed, you would get . . . $30,000. And your idea was for us to just get you your equity of $30,000 and you would deed the house over to us, is that right?

Seller: Yeah, I just want what's coming to me and then to walk.

Investor: Boy, I can sure understand that. An idea comes to mind, you'll probably think it's crazy, but what if we were willing to buy the property and make up the back payments, spend all the time and money to fix it up, and then sell it right away? And when we resell the property a few months from now, we'd get you a cashier's check for $30,000. The reason I even bring this up is that this way we can keep the cash in the deal to around $40,000, which makes it much easier for me to convince my partner that this is a good deal for us. [*We couldn't resist throwing a little higher authority in for good measure.*] But you probably think this is crazy, that you'd rather just keep on selling it yourself, huh?

Seller: No, I don't think it's crazy. I can understand that you're trying to make this a good deal for you too. How am I going to make sure I get paid my $30,000?

Investor: That's a really good point. I'm guessing that your idea was to make sure you secure yourself with the paperwork that requires us to pay you your money before we can sell the house to our buyer. That is important for you and I'm glad you brought that up. I would have if I were you. Yeah, so we'll make sure we get a deed of trust in place to protect you just like you were the bank. Not to mention all the money that we're going to have to put in here to fix up the house before we resell it.

Seller: Good, I just wanted to make sure that I was covered.

Investor: Of course. Now I just want to make sure I have it all clear. What you said you wanted us to do was to buy the house and make up the back payments, signing that deed of trust to require us to get you your $30,000 before we can sell it to our buyer, then we'll fix up the house and then sell it as quickly as possible so we both get paid. Did I get what you had said right?

When it comes to spending psychological currency, don't be stingy! Give the seller credit wherever you can. Did you notice *five* specific places in the negotiating transcript where we gave the seller credit for coming up with a good idea or ownership of an answer in the negotiation that let the seller feel smart (one form of psychological payoff)? Go back over this conversation until you can spot all five instances of giving the seller psychological currency.

#5. Talking (and Thinking) Too Fast

Sometimes investors forget to play the "reluctant" role by talking too fast. This can really put the seller on guard and create a barrier to emotionally connecting with the seller.

Here are three quick techniques to make sure you don't fall victim to this pitfall:

1. Slow down—always make sure your pace of speech is just a bit slower than the seller you are negotiating with. People instinctively associate fast-talkers with wheeler-dealers and sharpie investors.

2. Adopt a passive posture—round off your shoulders, let your stomach relax, lower your head. Why? Because alert, angular body posture and sharp, fast movements and gestures make it difficult for a seller to relax and feel comfortable being open with you. This also softens your voice and mutes the energy you send off, which in turn relaxes the seller even more.

3. Special warning for men: The two previous points are ten times as critical for you than for women. If you're negotiating with a woman, you have to put her at ease and not intimidate her. For example, this means being respectful by not standing or sitting too close to her, and talking in a soft voice and manner. With other men, you'll have to be cautious not to butt heads. Let the man you're negotiating with feel physically comfortable by using the other two techniques. You'll negotiate a much more profitable deal by neutralizing the danger of getting into an ego battle.

#6. Not Letting the Seller Save Face by "Winning" at Parts of the Negotiation

In your negotiation, look for places where you can help sellers feel like they've won. Sellers have to be able to face their families and neighbors, not to mention themselves. Help them be winners.

#7. Using Impressive Language That Intimidates the Seller

The final mistake is using jargon and technical language with the sellers. While it might feel good for you to use words such as *subject to* and *wholesaling* and *assigning,* we caution you about using them. Remember, in any negotiation there are two payoffs. Talking in impressive language will give you the psychological payoff, but will oftentimes kill a deal. It makes sellers feel less intelligent, more confused, and more intimidated. Instead, always talk in descriptive language that immediately makes sense to the seller.

Here are two quick examples:

Example one:

Investor: What if we were to make up the back payments and buy the house? Then we'd just take over making the payment each month. Is this something we should even talk about, or you probably hate the idea, huh? [*You just offered to buy the house subject to the existing financing.*]

Example two:

Investor: Well, I'm not sure if this is even going to be a fit for me. I'm having a hard time imagining I could even get my partner to go along with this. But what if I could get my partner to agree to get you the $100,000 cash—would you be open to talking about waiting 60 to 120 days, maybe 180 days at the most, to get that $100,000? We'd need this time to complete the renovation on the property and find a buyer to get us both cashed out of the property. Should we even talk about this option or probably not? [*You just offered to do a short-term "subject to" deal and cash out the seller by reselling the house to a retail cash buyer as soon as possible.*]

You now have a complete system for negotiating with sellers. This Five-Step framework took us years to create. All these ideas have been tested in the real world and have been proven to work, making investors like you a lot of money. Give yourself some time to integrate these negotiating ideas into your investing; return to this chapter again and again to refine your technique. The payoff is worth the investment you put in because negotiation is one of the most important investing skills you can ever develop.

24 Foreclosure Pitfalls That Can Cost You Big!

This chapter shows you how to avoid the major pitfalls of buying from sellers in foreclosure. It draws heavily from our own deals (especially the ones that went bad) so you can shortcut your learning curve. We learned about all 24 of these pitfalls the hard way; we share them here to help you profit from our painful experiences.

Pitfall #1: Letting the Seller Stay in the House

At some point in your foreclosure career, probably on your first or second house, you are going to be tempted to let a seller stay in the property after you have purchased his home. After all, he is in such a bad place and he has such a nice family and they only need a few weeks to find another place to move into . . .

When that time comes, we urge you to come back to this section of the book and read the following words of advice. (As a matter of fact, put a note next to this section so that you can make it easier to find when you need it most.) Here is that advice:

Never, ever let the sellers stay in the property once you have purchased the property.

Can we be serious? Deadly serious. If you let the sellers stay in the property, you are asking for trouble. Either they won't find another place or they will keep coming up with reason after reason, excuse after excuse, story after story about why they need more time. And when you ask them to leave they'll get angry with you, as if you were the one who caused them to stop making payments to their lender. All the while, if you're not careful, this is eating into your profits, and potentially into your own checkbook. This point is so important, and so often ignored, that we've incorporated some subtle variations on this theme in the next pitfall.

Pitfall #2: Renting the Property Back to the Seller

You will find many sellers who tell you they will sell you their house if only they can rent the property back from you. While they'll promise to take great care of the house and the numbers will look good on paper, don't do it!

We understand that it seems like the deal won't work unless you give in on this point, but there is usually a better solution if you really put your collective minds to it. Blame it on your partner so you can still maintain your rapport with the seller, but be very firm on this point—your partner won't let you buy the property unless the seller moves.

Just think for a moment. If the sellers can't make their house payments, how are they going to pay you rent? And if they don't pay you the rent and you move to evict them, just imagine the nightmare of having to deal with them getting more and more upset and rewriting the history of how you bought the property. The real history may have had you playing the role of hero, but we can guarantee you'll get cast in a more sinister role in this revised version. When the emotions get charged, sometimes the rational mind gets shut off.

■ **David's Story**

I once bought a house from a couple who were a few weeks away from the trustee's sale date. They gave me a big discount on the price in exchange for a fast sale. I clarified the amount they would net after paying their share of the closing costs. They left me several voice-mail messages expressing their gratitude for helping them, and they reaffirmed the rough amount they would walk away from the sale with. Because the sellers hadn't found another place to live in yet, they asked to rent back the property for up to three months. We talked this over and they even agreed to have the three months' rent, plus a security deposit, escrowed directly from their proceeds from the sale. Like a dummy I agreed, thinking this time it would be different. (And I knew better!)

A few days after the closing, I started getting angry calls from this couple. They accused me of cheating them even though they netted the amount of money I'd told them they would. They damaged the property, upset all the neighbors, and screamed to everyone who was within earshot how terrible a person I was. I found this upsetting, to say the least. Over time I came to realize that some people who find themselves in rough times need to lash out. Yes, it is amazing how fast people's minds change, but remember, they're not bad people, they're just in a bad place. The best advice I can give you is to be straight with every seller so you can maintain your own sense of integrity and make vacating the property a condition of the sale.   ■

One "technique" used by some investors is to buy a foreclosure from a seller and rent it back to the seller with an option to buy the property back at a significantly higher price. The investor stops the foreclosure by making up the back payments. From the investor's perspective, either the seller exercises his option to buy the property back at a healthy profit to the investor, or the seller doesn't, in which case the investor keeps the house with its built-in profit. In most cases, the seller can't make the rent payments and the investor has to evict the seller.

Not only do you have all the emotional hassles of this process, but you also have a lot of legal liability from the way the deal is structured. Technically, in many states a seller could claim that you didn't buy the property from him but merely lent him the money he needed to stop the foreclosure. And because your "profit" (as built in by the much higher option price you gave back to him) could make your rate of return on the money you "lent" him by making up back payments higher than the state-allowed maximum, you could be guilty of usury. As crazy as this may seem to you, this is a real possibility in many states. Our advice is to avoid structuring your deal this way. If, however, you feel you want to do this, we urge you to talk with an experienced real estate attorney about the legal implications in your county and state.

Pitfall #3: Putting *Serious* Money in the Deal before the Seller Vacates

We recommend that you never give sellers a large chunk of money before they have moved out of the property. This is your only real form of leverage to ensure that they do in fact live up to their word and move out. Just what is "serious money"? This varies from investor to investor. Our definition of serious money is any amount of money that would cause you to pause before walking away from the deal. For some investors this might by a few hundred dollars, for others a few thousand.

We also recommend that you hold up making all the back payments or investing serious money in the fix-up work until the sellers have moved out. If you do start investing heavily in the property, then with each dollar you spend, you become more committed to the deal and it becomes even harder for you to maintain the emotional detachment to intelligently deal with any risks that come when the seller refuses to move out. The bottom line is that you only put serious money into properties that are keeper deals and you only have a keeper deal if the seller has moved out.

Pitfall #4: Giving Sellers All Their Money *before* the Final Walk-Through

Make sure you take the time to walk through the property before you hand over that final check to the seller. Don't worry whether the property is clean or dirty; you are going to hire a professional cleaning service anyway. Instead check for big things like damage to the property. Did the sellers leave the appliances (if that was part of the agreement)? You want to protect yourself from the shock of any unpleasant surprises.

Pitfall #5: Putting Serious Money in the Deal before Completing Your Due Diligence

The more money you have in a deal, the more you have to lose. Remember that any foreclosure deal may unravel after you conduct your due diligence. Make sure you haven't committed to the deal by putting in more money than you are comfortable walking away from.

In *Making Big Money Investing in Real Estate,* we go into great detail about the seven steps of your due diligence (pages 149–164). We encourage you to read through that section for our Due Diligence Checklist and our step-by-step comprehensive guide. We're going to share some insights that add to your due diligence in the next several pitfalls—especially important when you're buying foreclosures. Here are two of them:

1. Talk with neighbors to get the REAL story.
2. Carefully read all the seller's loan paperwork on any "subject to" deal.

Talk With Neighbors to Get the REAL Story

Often, neighbors are motivated to help you buy the property— they don't like the fact that their house is worth less because of the eyesore next door or they're uncomfortable that the foreclosure situation will negatively impact their neighborhood.

They can often tell you the history of the house, any repair problems it's had, and much more. Some people hide information because they really want you to buy and fix up the property. But you'll find enough honest ones that, if you're a good listener, they'll tell you the inside story on the seller's situation and the history of the house. They can also give you valuable information on property values and trends, neighborhood concerns, and what's going on— good and bad—in the local area.

Carefully Read All the Seller's Loan Paperwork on Any "Subject to" Deal

Always get copies of the actual loan documents from the seller. Read through these documents very carefully, especially the actual promissory note and deed of trust/mortgage. Sometimes sellers can mislead you about the terms or conditions of the loan. While rarely will they lie outright, many times they can be mistaken on the information they give you. If they don't have the paperwork anymore, contact their lender and have them fax or mail you a duplicate copy.

■ **Peter's Story**

We bought a $125,000 house a few years back from a seller who just couldn't make the payments anymore. We made up five back payments and took over the property subject to the existing financing, which we thought was at a 7.9 percent fixed rate for 30 years. It turned out that the loan was an ARM—an adjustable rate mortgage. We got lucky because interest rates had dropped, but it could just have easily turned out the opposite with interest rates climbing and the higher payment cutting into our positive cash flow. I know it's time-consuming, but if you are buying subject to, take the time to look over the seller's loan documents.   ■

Pitfall #6: Not Accurately Determining the Real Market Value of the Property

Make sure you take the time to conservatively calculate the market value of the property. There are *two* market values to check—the resale value and the market rental value.

Checking the "Comps"

It's important to know the market rental value of a property if you plan to sell it to an investor or if you plan to hang on to the property over time. The way property values are determined for single-family houses is by finding out what other similar (or comparable) houses in the area have sold for in the recent past. What this means is that a three-bedroom, two-bath, 1,850-square-foot house is probably worth what other comparable houses have sold for in a given area. Obviously, for two properties to be comparable, they need to have:

- Similar square footage (ideally within 200 square feet or less)
- Same number of bedrooms and bathrooms
- Similar construction type and condition, etc.
- Same school districts/county

This is a simplification of the process of determining value. It takes time to learn how to value a home and it's a skill you will learn. In the beginning, if you sign up a deal, latch onto a good real estate agent in the area who can help you determine its value. As a backup, you can always hire a professional appraiser for the first house or two you buy.

Checking Market Rents: Rent Survey

A rent survey is an analysis of what properties similar to the one you have under contract are renting for. While you might not be able to determine to the dollar just what this value is, you almost always will be able to determine a range of rents. It's important for you to know the market rent value of a property if you plan to sell it to an investor or if you plan to hold onto the property over time.

Pitfall #7: Not Checking the Title Carefully Enough

One of the biggest dangers in a foreclosure deal is that you aren't getting *marketable title* to the property you are buying. Marketable title means your ownership claim to the property is so strong that you can easily sell the property to a buyer who will bring in conventional financing, which requires a title insurance policy. The title must be free of any consequential clouds, whether they are actual or merely potential. That's just a fancy way of saying there can't be any liens or claims against the title that would scare a title company into listing these title glitches as "exemptions" to a title insurance policy. Otherwise you would have significant trouble selling the property to a cash buyer. You'll learn more about title insurance in the next pitfall. For the moment, you are going to have to get a title company to give you a title report, also known as an *ownership and encumbrance* report. This will show you all the liens against the property.

Checking Title Items

Here are ten items to check the chain of title for:

1. County tax liens for nonpayment of property taxes
2. Homeowner association liens for fees owed or special assessments that are unpaid
3. Other taxing authorities' liens (city, state, or federal)
4. Mortgages (first, second, third . . .)
5. Local utility company liens (e.g., for unpaid water and sewage bills)
6. Judgments from any creditors
7. Mechanics' liens
8. Other people on title (e.g., son listed on title as joint tenant)
9. Spouse or ex-spouse, including community property rights (more on this in Pitfall #11)
10. Heirs of the previous owner who might have a claim to the title

Pitfall #8: Not Buying Title Insurance If You Put Serious Money in the Deal

Title insurance is a form of insurance that protects you from any prior claim or cloud on the property title that happened *before* you bought it. This just might be the only type of insurance that insures against past events. Basically, when you buy title insurance, you are paying the title company to thoroughly research the chain of title. The title insurance company issues a report that lists any "exclusions" to the policy. It's critical to carefully check this part. Make sure you're either comfortable with each item or you clear up any items in question before you close. If a claim arises that the title insurance company didn't list as an exclusion and it ends up costing you money later, the title insurance company will pay out money on that claim. As with any insurance, limitations exist, so have the title company explain them to you.

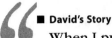

■ **David's Story**

When I put any real money into a property, I always buy title insurance. This might cost me several hundred dollars, but my peace of mind is more than worth it. I also recommend purchasing insurance for all your foreclosure deals, unless you are an experienced investor who's willing and able to intelligently take on the risk of not buying it.   ■

Pitfall #9: Not Running a Credit Check on the Seller

Make sure you get sellers to sign a permission form to allow you to run a credit check on them. You'll need their Social Security numbers to run this credit report. Taking this extra step of running a credit check can save you a lot of heartache down the line.

What to Look for on the Seller's Credit Report

- Credit history that indicates a current or pending bankruptcy (see Pitfall #10)
- Marital status—important if you live in a community property state (see Pitfall #11)
- Any other creditors who may have claims to the property

Pitfall #10: Seller Declaring a Bankruptcy

A seller can file two types of bankruptcy:

1. Chapter 13 bankruptcy (restructuring)—where the court imposes a forced payment plan on all creditors seeking payment.
2. Chapter 7 Bankruptcy (absolving debts)—where most types of debts are canceled.

You are probably asking, "What happens if the seller declares bankruptcy? How does this affect the foreclosure process?" While many sellers think this will stop a foreclosure, they are wrong. The best sellers can hope for is a delay (typically a month or two) of the foreclosure until the lender petitions the court to release the property from the bankruptcy so that the lender can get on with the foreclosure process. The cost to the sellers is that their credit will be even worse with bankruptcy and foreclosure than with just foreclosure.

If the sellers have already declared bankruptcy before the sale, you will need the Bankruptcy Trustee's permission to allow the sale. This should not be a problem as long as the sellers aren't making a profit and you aren't getting too good of a deal. If you are, the Trustee may feel that you are getting equity that should in all fairness go to creditors.

The biggest risk you have to protect yourself from if the seller declares bankruptcy is something called *fraudulent conveyance.* This is a legal term that means that the seller didn't have the right to transfer the property to you because he was defrauding his creditors who rightfully should have gotten the equity in the property. This probably won't be an issue, as long as the seller didn't have much equity. The seller's creditors would actually have to file suit for fraudulent conveyance and prove that you knew of the seller's debts and received too good of a deal in a way that wasn't fair to the creditors. If a court agrees with the fraudulent conveyance claim, the sale can be set aside for up to two years. Our best advice is to make sure you talk with a highly skilled attorney if you are buying a property from a seller who either has declared or is about to declare a bankruptcy.

Pitfall #11: Only Buying Half a House

If you are investing in a community property state, then regardless of who is technically on the recorded deed, current or past spouses probably have an interest in that property. You'll have to protect yourself by getting both spouses to sign all important documents, such as the purchase contract and deed. Make sure that you get every signature notarized; sellers have been known to forge their ex-spouses' signatures. Check to make sure the notary lists *both* sellers' names on the acknowledgment, and thus notarized both persons' identities and signatures, and didn't just notarize one signature (with the other signature forged later).

Another way to protect yourself is by getting a signed and notarized Quitclaim Deed from the other spouse or ex-spouse deeding any interest he has in the property over to you. Or he can quitclaim his interest over to his spouse or ex-spouse who then can sell you the property.

Community Property States

Here's a list of community property states:

- California
- Nevada
- Louisiana
- Texas

- Wisconsin
- Idaho
- Arizona
- New Mexico
- Washington

Also, ask a good attorney in your area about "palimony claims." Similar to community property claims, these arise when a couple has lived together for so long that they may be seen as a common-law married couple.

Pitfall #12: Not Getting the Property Professionally Inspected

You need to know what you are getting yourself into. Hire a professional inspector and make sure you take the time to go over what the inspector has found so that you are making an intelligent decision about moving forward on the deal.

We don't recommend you act as your own inspector for two reasons. First, your time can be better spent by staying in the investor role, which is a more highly paid role than that of property inspector. Second, it's too easy in your excitement over what a great deal you are getting to overlook a problem that an objective inspector would catch.

Pitfall #13: Messing Up Your Paperwork

While you will probably need legal help on your first few deals, fairly soon you'll be able to handle most of the closing paperwork yourself. Not only will this save you time and money, but it will also give you an extra degree of control in the closing process. Even if you use an outside escrow or title company to perform your real estate closings, by knowing how to prepare the documents yourself you will be able to more intelligently use these closing agents' services.

Checking Your Paperwork

Three critical items to check on your paperwork include:

1. The owner's exact name and spelling on the title. Make sure that the name on the deed and other paperwork is the same as the name on the deed through which the sellers gained title when they bought the property. If the owner is a corporation, limited liability company, or a trustee of a trust, make sure you see the written documentation that authorizes the seller to transfer title to you on behalf of this other entity.

2. The correct *legal description* of the property. This is the fancy "official" address used to accurately identify the property. It usually looks like, "Lot 3, Block 5 of Sunny Side Acres Subdivision as recorded on Map No. 2377, page 744 as recorded . . ." You can copy this from the old deed or from the title report. Take care to get it right, or you will have problems later. We recommend you double-check it, then check it *backwards*—letter by letter, space by space—one time. Then get someone else to triple-check it, letter by letter, space by space.

3. Use the right deed (or a deed normal for your area). Get a copy of a deed from a local title company that your county's land records or Recorder's Office *is used to seeing*. You want the documents you plan on recording, like the deeds and Memorandum of Agreements, to be formatted just like the other documents that the recorder's office is used to seeing. This will help you avoid any title problems when

you resell the property. Remember, to have marketable title, a title insurance company must be comfortable with the chain of title. If the deed you used to acquire title to the property is out of the ordinary, it will wave a red flag at the title insurance representative who is working on the title policy. You can easily avoid this by taking a little extra time to make sure your deeds and other recorded documents fit the format that is primarily used in your area.

Pitfall #14: Not Following Your State's Foreclosure Laws

Some states have specific laws about how investors must interact with sellers who are in foreclosure. Make sure you study the laws in your area so you follow them at all times. (To save you many hours of research, we've included links to many of the important laws in a state-by-state listing included in "Your Bonus Web Pack" at the end of the book.)

For example, California is probably the toughest state for laws outlining what an investor can and cannot do. In California, anytime an investor buys a property from a seller who is in foreclosure (i.e., the Notice of Default has been filed), the investor must give the seller a five-day right of rescission. During this time, the investor is not allowed to get the seller to sign any type of deed or pay the seller any money. If the investor breaks these rules (or other rules of the state), then the sale can be turned aside at any point in the next two *years!* So make sure you carefully read the section in "Your Web Bonus Pack" in the back of this book that deals with these critical laws.

Pitfall #15: Falling into the Insurance Trap

The insurance trap comes in three varieties. First, many investors who buy a property, especially if they are buying the property subject to the existing financing, forget to convert the existing homeowners policy into a landlord or rental property policy. Not that we're cynical about insurance companies using any type of technicality to get out of paying out a large claim, but we advise you not to give them a chance. Make sure when the seller is endorsing over the existing insurance policy that you have the policy changed to reflect that it's no longer an owner-occupied property.

Second, don't forget to remove the seller's name from the policy. It would be a real shame if you filed a claim and simply because you didn't remove the seller's name from the policy, his name appeared on the claim check!

Third, when buying a property subject to the existing financing, it's tempting to just take the seller's name from the policy and put in your name as the main insured party. The problem with this is that the existing mortgagee (the lender who lent the seller money to buy the property) is on the policy as the additionally insured party. As such, when the policy is changed in any way, this mortgagee will be notified. It doesn't take a rocket scientist at the bank to make the connection between there being a new main insured on the policy and the property being sold without the lender's permission. This could get you into trouble with a due-on-sale clause.

As we shared with the readers of our last book, there are two ways to handle this. One is to simply leave the first insurance policy in the name of the seller and go out and get a second policy naming you as the main insured. Yes, this will mean paying twice for insurance, but the cost isn't that much for the benefit of getting the property subject to the existing financing.

The second way to sidestep this insurance trap is by using a *land trust*. A land trust is simply a trust that is created to hold title of a property for the benefit of some beneficial party. Any seller may put his property into a land trust without violating the due-on-sale clause (this is federal law.) The seller merely deeds the property you are buying subject to the existing financing to a land trust naming himself as the beneficiary and you, the investor, as the trustee. Then in a separate document the seller assigns the beneficial interest of his land trust from himself to you. Now you become both the trustee (who controls the property) and the beneficiary (who gets all the benefits of the property.) For all practical purposes and for tax purposes you now own the property.

As for the due-on-sale clause when you do things this way, the act of the seller deeding the property into the land trust with himself as the beneficiary does *not* violate the due-on-sale clause. This deed from the seller to you as the trustee of the land trust gets recorded. You help the seller write a quick letter to the lender notifying it that the owner has put the property into trust for financial planning purposes and, from here on out, all correspondence about the loan should be with the trustee (who happens to be you, the investor). You give the lender your address in this letter as the trustee and from here on out you will be the lender's contact person on the loan. (Note: You still have zero liability for this loan!)

In a separate transaction (which can take place ten seconds after the previous one), the seller assigns over his beneficial interest in the land trust to you, the investor. While this could trigger the due-on-sale clause because the property title really is being transferred to you, the bank never knows about this transaction because this assignment is *never* recorded.

How does this help you with the insurance trap? You simply switch the policy from the seller to you as the trustee of the XWZ Property Trust. The lender expects and is used to this change. Everyone is happy—the bank, the seller, the insurance company, and you the investor. This is our preferred way of handling subject to deals. Once you do one this way, you'll find it really is fairly simple.

Pitfall #16: Seller Pushing the Loan to Get Called Due

While most sellers will respect their agreement to allow you to buy the property subject to the existing financing and to not do anything that would cause the lender to call the loan due, some sellers forget about their earlier promises. Several years later, they are no longer motivated sellers and they really want you to get that loan out of their name, usually so they can more easily finance the purchase of another property. A few of these sellers will even take the next step—to force your hand by calling up their old lenders and telling them that they have sold the house several years ago and that the lenders should call the loan due.

While you have no legal or financial obligation to pay off the loan if the lender does call it due, the lender could foreclose on the house and you would then lose out on your equity. While this may seem scary, we want to reassure you that it isn't a very likely occurrence. First, if you deal openly and intelligently with your seller up front, chances are very good that he will honor the agreement (more on this in a moment). Next, even if the lender does call the loan due, you can usually just assume the loan, sell the property to a new buyer, or refinance the property. Typically, if you are polite and open with the lender, you'll have four to eight months or more to do this.

Five Ways to Protect Yourself from the Seller Spilling the Beans

1. Make sure the seller understands at the start of the deal that if the lender finds out, which is unlikely unless the seller tells the lender, it could be costly for both the seller and the investor. Clearly state that the only reason this deal works for you as an investor is that the seller allows you to bring the old loan current and take over the payments each month. Ex-

plain that if you had to bring in your own financing, you would need to get a much lower price to offset the added expense of getting the new loan and the fact that it would tie up so much more of your investing capital.

2. Get a strong disclaimer from the seller that says she understands you are taking title subject to the loan(s) and what that means. The CYS, or cover yourself, addendum we use states that the seller *"will not commit any action or make any statement orally or in writing that will cause the existing lender(s) to discover that title has been transferred."*

3. Make sure you live up to all your commitments to the seller. One reason she might call up her lender is if an unscrupulous investor didn't do what he promised.

4. Make sure you coach the seller on what to do if the lender writes or calls her. You don't want a problem caused simply out of ignorance. Ask her to forward all lender mail to you (in fact, have her sign a change of address letter to the lender asking the lender to send all correspondence about the loan to your address). If the lender calls, train the seller to be "busy" and not talk with the lender until you have talked with her on the phone.

5. Owe the seller money. Nothing keeps a seller living up to her promises like you having the leverage of owing her money. This is not to say you should overpay for the property just to owe the seller money, but if you have to pay her money, see if you can make some of it payable down the road.

Pitfall #17: Seller Disappearing Once You've Bought the Property and You Need a Signature

The best way to cover yourself on this risk is to get the seller to sign a *limited power of attorney* that authorizes you to sign on the seller's behalf on all matters concerning this one specific property. (For more details, including a sample copy of a limited power of attorney form, see *Making Big Money Investing in Real Estate,* pages 73–75.)

Pitfall #18: Having Liability Even When You Assign Your Contract

If you choose to flip your deal to another investor for a fast cash profit, make sure you get a signed release from both the buyer and the seller. Also, if your contract with the seller allowed you to buy the property subject to the existing financing, make sure you require that your assignee (the investor you're selling the deal to) signs a wraparound mortgage or an All-Inclusive Trust Deed to protect the seller. (You'll learn about these in Chapter 8.) Finally, be willing to step back in if the assignee ever defaults (ask your seller to save your contact information so he can call you if ever the assignee is more than 30 days late in making payments). Not only is this the right thing to do, but it's also good business—you just might profit from the house twice!

Pitfall #19: Seller Claiming Duress

Whenever you're buying a property from a seller in foreclosure, you're buying from someone in a vulnerable position. While you will operate with integrity, be careful that a bitter seller who's mad at the world doesn't make claims stating you forced him into the deal.

To protect yourself, always operate at arm's length in the deal. Don't demand that the seller deed the property to you on your first visit or refuse to allow the seller to have an advisor at the closing. Make sure you encourage the seller to make his decision independently and to invite a third-party advisor to any meetings you have if the seller wants that advisor there.

Also, include a clause like the following in your purchase contract and ask the seller to initial it:

> *Seller hereby acknowledges that all negotiations and dealings with the Buyer have been and are at arm's length and that no duress or undue influence has been exerted by Buyer on Seller or any member of Seller's family in connection with this purchase and sale of this Property.*

Pitfall #20: Seller Claiming Misrepresentation

Because the seller is under stress, you must protect yourself from the seller coming back later, claiming you tricked him into making the deal by misrepresenting certain things.

The simplest way to protect yourself is to put everything you and the seller agree on in writing. Also, follow up every important phone conversation with a letter explaining what both parties discussed and agreed to (see Pitfall #23 for more on this point). We recommend that you include in your final contract a "merger" clause stating this agreement is the full and final expression of exactly what you and the seller did and did not agree to.

Here's the legalese version of a merger clause:

> *This agreement represents the full and final understanding between the parties. No agreements or representations, unless specifically incorporated into this agreement, shall be binding upon any of the parties.*

Here's another clause that we encourage you to put in your agreement with the seller:

> *Seller understands and is aware that the present fair market value of the Property is probably much higher than the purchase price set forth in this agreement. Seller hereby expressly waives any and all claims to potential or actual profit, income, or other sums in excess of the amount stated above in this agreement that comes from the Buyer reselling the property or Buyer's rights under this agreement. Furthermore, Seller hereby acknowledges that the purchase price stated herein is fair and equitable and is in the Seller's best interests, and that the Seller's decision to sell was based on the Seller and that the Seller has not relied on any representation(s) of Buyer that is (are) not expressly contained in this agreement.*

(For more information on how you can get all the contracts and agreements we use in our investing on CD-ROM, see "Your Bonus Web Pack" at the back of the book.)

Pitfall #21: Seller Backing Out of the Deal

If the sellers want out of the deal for valid reasons and within a reasonable period of time (up to three days after signing the deal), let them gracefully out of it. If, however, they want to back out of the deal because, two weeks later, they got a better offer from another investor, that's not fair to you. In this case, we recommend you hold them to the deal. In fact, we recommend that if the sellers ever want to back out of the deal after a few days and if you've spent significant money or time working on it, you make them pay you something to cancel the agreement. That's being fair to both of you.

To protect yourself from sellers backing out, make sure you always record a Memorandum of Agreement (see Figure 6.1) against

---

FIGURE 6.1   Memorandum of Agreement

RECORDING REQUESTED BY:

WHEN RECORDED MAIL AND UNLESS OTHERWISE
SHOWN BELOW, MAIL TAX STATEMENTS TO:

SPACE ABOVE THIS LINE FOR RECORDER'S USE

Memorandum of Agreement

Be the world hereby apprised that I/we _____ (Obligor)
have entered into an agreement with _____
(Obligee) wherein the Obligor has agreed to sell the below described property to the
Obligee:

<<PropertyLegal>>.

Anyone dealing in and with the subject property should contact Obligee at:

_____

regarding the terms of this purchase agreement and the parties' respective rights
thereunder. IN WITNESS WHEREOF, the parties have signed this agreement.

Dated _____

STATE OF _____)
COUNTY OF _____) S.S.

On _____ before me,   _____

_____ ,   Obligor   Date

personally appeared _____

_____ ,   _____

personally known to me (or proved to me on the basis   Obligor   Date
of satisfactory evidence) to be the person(s) whose
name(s) is/are subscribed to the within instrument and
acknowledged to me that he/she/they executed the same
in his/her/their authorized capacity(ies) and that by
his/her/their signature(s) on the instrument the
person(s), or the entity upon behalf of which the
person(s) acted, executed the instrument.

WITNESS my hand and official seal.

Signature _____

MAIL TAX STATEMENTS AS DIRECTED ABOVE

MY COMMISSION EXPIRES:

---

the property if you don't close within two days. A better way to close on the property quickly is by having the seller deed you the house subject to existing financing. Insist that you still have the option of backing out of the deal if, after your due diligence, you discover something you don't like.

In the event you do back out of the deal, make sure you put down in writing that you can simply quitclaim the property back to the seller and cancel the agreement with no further liability.

■ **David's Story**

I was buying a house from a highly motivated seller with John, one of our Mentorship program's real estate coaches. I was so busy in the office that I delayed the closing for two weeks to complete another project. The night before the closing, I spent about two hours drawing up all the documents and getting ready for the closing to be held at my office at 9 AM the following day. The next day, the seller showed up right on time, only to tell me he'd found another solution to his problem. While I talked with the seller about how much he was willing to pay me to let him out of the agreement, all I kept thinking was that *this was my fault.* I never should have waited 14 days to close. I should have closed a few days after we signed the deal and just made it clear we wouldn't make payments on the house for 30 days or so.

The moral to the story is that when you have a motivated seller ready to deed the property over to you—let him do it immediately. And then, with your name on the title, conduct your due diligence before you invest any serious money into the deal.   ■

Pitfall #22: Investing in Your Own Name

In today's litigious world, you're taking your financial life in your own hands if you invest without at least one layer of liability protection in place. For the average investor, that means forming a limited liability company (LLC) and always operating from behind that protective screen. This is even more important if you are starting your investing business with significant assets you've already accumulated such as a pension, a business you own, a personal residence with a lot of equity, or other rental properties you own. Invest the time not only in forming a limited liability company or corporation to protect yourself, but in learning how to operate it so it's properly maintained. Hold annual meetings, with members' resolutions, and never commingle funds. (You'll find more information on the best ways to protect your assets in "Your Web Bonus Pack" at the back of the book.)

Pitfall #23: Not Papering Your Trail

After a while, all deals look alike and the details, no matter how clear they were in the beginning, start to blur. Make sure you meticulously document each deal. This includes logging in every conversation you hold with your seller and your buyer or renter. Note the date and time you talked along with the important items you discussed. While this seems like a lot of effort, and it is, you'll enjoy the peace of mind that comes from knowing, and being able to prove, that you've lived up to all your agreements with others.

Start a business journal in which you keep notes from all your conversations. Also, log in all phone messages along with what the other parties said. Finally, consider using follow-up letters to clarify the main points you discussed and to establish a clear paper trail of what was agreed on.

Pitfall #24: Taking Personal Responsibility for Seller's Situation

All investors must find the right balance between caring about the seller, yet not taking on responsibility for the seller's situation. You can't help the seller by being a philanthropist. First and foremost, you're running a business. While you're committed to "win-win or no deal," this doesn't mean you can "save" every seller. In fact, you shouldn't try to save the seller at all.

We've watched many investors struggle trying to help a seller when the numbers just can't be made to work. Be careful of win-lose negotiating in which you sacrifice your need to make a profit to help a seller. In the end, this type of negotiating only makes things worse because you won't be able to live up to your side of the agreement.

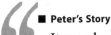

■ **Peter's Story**

It was hard for me early on; I just wanted to "save" every seller I met. I finally came to realize that while I could always empathize with them and hear them out, I wasn't willing to step over the line and take their situation on my back. That wouldn't be fair to me or my family. Plus, it would mean I couldn't help other sellers because I'd soon be out of business.

The place I settled into was one of listening respectfully and compassionately. I would clearly let the seller know where I stood in the deal from the start. If I don't see a way to make a profit in the deal, I tell the seller up front that it won't be a fit for me, then I give her some helpful suggestions about what she can do. Not only does this help me keep my investing business in balance with my family and other commitments, but sellers appreciate the up-front manner with which I work with them.   ■

So there are all 24 foreclosure pitfalls and how you can safely sidestep them. Use them as a guide to help you navigate the sometimes perilous world of foreclosure investing. Here's a list of the 24 pitfalls:

- Pitfall #1: Letting the seller stay in the house
- Pitfall #2: Renting the property back to the seller

- Pitfall #3: Putting *serious* money in the deal before the seller vacates
- Pitfall #4: Giving sellers all their money *before* the final walk-through
- Pitfall #5: Putting serious money in the deal before completing due diligence
- Pitfall #6: Not accurately determining the real market value of the property
- Pitfall #7: Not checking the title carefully enough
- Pitfall #8: Not buying title insurance if you put serious money in the deal
- Pitfall #9: Not running a credit check on the seller
- Pitfall #10: Seller declaring a bankruptcy
- Pitfall #11: Only buying half a house
- Pitfall #12: Not getting the property professionally inspected
- Pitfall #13: Messing up your paperwork
- Pitfall #14: Not following your state's foreclosure laws
- Pitfall #15: Falling into the insurance trap
- Pitfall #16: Seller pushing the loan to get called due
- Pitfall #17: Seller disappearing once you've bought the property and you need a signature
- Pitfall #18: Having liability even when you assign your contract
- Pitfall #19: Seller claiming duress
- Pitfall #20: Seller claiming misrepresentation
- Pitfall #21: Seller backing out of the deal
- Pitfall #22: Investing in your own name
- Pitfall #23: Not papering your trail
- Pitfall #24: Taking personal responsibility for seller's situation

Use these 24 pitfalls to help you navigate the perilous world of foreclosure investing. As part of "Your Bonus Web Pack" at the end of the book, we've included a special report titled "Final Deal Checklist—the 27 Questions You Must Ask Before You Move Forward on Any Deal." This special report may be downloaded for free. It will help you take one last look at any deal and help assure you it's a smart move to go forward with.

In the next chapter, you'll learn how to turn your deals into quick cash profits. This is especially important if you want to use your foreclosure investing to generate immediate cash flow.

How to Flip Your Deals for Quick Cash Profits

Before we discuss how to turn your deals for quick cash profits, let's recap all the ways you can make money with any real estate deal.

Seven Profit Centers in Your Deal

1. *Cash flow.* This is simply the difference between the income the property generates and the expenses it costs.
2. *Amortization.* This fancy word means the equity pay-down of the underlying loan(s) on the property. Each time you pay the lender on most loans, a portion goes toward principal and a chunk pays the interest. Over time, you pay the loan down to zero and own the property free and clear. This is called the amortization of the loan.
3. *Tax benefits.* One of the last remaining tax breaks for the average person is real estate. You get to write off the interest paid, insurance, real estate taxes, and, best of all, depreciation.

4. *Appreciation.* Over time, most property goes up in value. And while this is usually a cyclical phenomenon, in just about every area of the country, this cycle keeps going higher and higher. In fact, the average rate of appreciation on a national average over the past 40 years was more than 6 percent. You can make a fortune when you combine this increase of value with your leveraging into a property using other people's money or other people's loans.

5. *Buying below value.* Because you'll be buying many of your foreclosures at bargain prices, another profit center will come from skillfully negotiating price.

6. *Discounting debt.* As discussed in Chapter 3, sometimes you can make extra money by getting lien holders or creditors to take less than they're owed as full payment, thus building more profit into the deal for yourself.

7. *Forfeited nonrefundable deposits and option payments.* When people you've sold a property to (or at least taken a nonrefundable deposit from to hold the property) back out of the deal, you may make several thousand dollars extra by keeping their nonrefundable payment to you. (More on this in Chapter 8.)

Depending on which exit strategy you use with your property, you'll be able to tap into some or even all of the profit centers you've just learned about. In this chapter, you'll learn how to turn your deal for a fast cash profit. In the next chapter, you'll learn how to structure your properties for maximum long-term wealth accumulation.

How to Flip or Wholesale Deals for Instant Cash Flow

You've already learned from Chapter 3 that you can sell deals you don't want to keep. This means either selling the contract for a cash *assignment fee* or selling the house quickly to a retail buyer. Let's get into the specific steps needed to make this happen.

Step One: Lock Up the Property Under Contract

Before you can ever flip a deal, you need to sign an agreement to buy that property from the seller. By applying all the marketing and negotiating strategies you've already learned, you'll find many deals to put under contract. Some you'll hang on to for the long term; others you'll sell for a quick profit.

You'll be signing up and selling two types of deals to other investors—cash deals or terms deals. With cash deals, you'll negotiate a discounted cash price, typically 60 percent to 70 percent of the "as is" value, in exchange for the seller getting all the cash at the closing. For example, imagine you met a seller who owned a $300,000 house that needed $20,000 of repairs. The seller can't make her monthly payment, let alone fix up her house. So you negotiate a sale price with the seller of $190,000 cash. You're thrilled since your price is 68 percent of the "as is" value. (The "as is" value is the after-repair value [ARV] of the property minus the cost of the work that needs to be done on the house to make it salable at that ARV.)

But you don't want to do the rehab or find the $190,000. Instead, you simply sell the deal to another investor who specializes in rehabs in your area. This new investor pays you $15,000 cash for you to assign your contract to him. Then he moves forward and buys the house from the seller. Once you have assigned your contract to the new investor and collected your $15,000 check, that's it. The investor you sold the deal to will do the rehab project and net $50,000 or more when reselling the property to a retail buyer (see Figure 7.1). Everyone wins.

FIGURE 7.1   Sample Numbers of Wholesaling Cash Deal

Step One: You Sign Up the Deal

After-repair value (ARV)	$300,000
"As is" value (ARV less repair costs)	$280,000
Your price	$190,000

Step Two: You Assign Your Contract to Another Investor

Your contract price	$190,000
Assignment fee you collect	$ 15,000
New investor's price	$205,000
Your net profit	$ 15,000

Step Three: You're Done . . . New Investor Rehabs, Then Resells the Property

ARV	$300,000
New investor's price	($205,000)
Repair cost	($ 20,000)
Closing costs	($ 3,000)
Holding costs	($ 4,000)
Commission when selling	($ 18,000)
New investor's net profit	$ 50,000

A terms deal is a deal in which either the seller is agreeing to wait for a period of time to get some or all of her equity, or in which little money goes to the seller. For example, imagine that same seller in the previous example owed $240,000 against the property. This time, you negotiated to buy the property for $245,000 by paying the seller $5,000 cash and taking title subject to the seller's existing $240,000 loan. And this time, you have a contract to purchase that house for 88 percent of the "as is" value, but you have great financing in place because you are buying subject to the seller's loan. Again you decide that you don't want to hang on to this deal but want to turn it for a fast profit. So you find a local investor willing to pay $10,000 to buy this deal from you. You make a fast $10,000 and your investor gets a deal that only requires $15,000 down and has long-term financing in place in the form of the seller's existing loan. Again, everyone wins.

Whether you sign up a cash deal or a terms deal, typically you can flip both types and turn a cash profit in 30 to 60 days. Here are the formulas to guide you as you determine how much to sell your deal for. With a cash deal, look to lock up the property for as low a price as possible, but make sure you're agreeing to pay *no more* than 65 percent to 70 percent of the "as is" value. Typically, you'll be able to find an investor to buy the property for between 70 percent and 80 percent of the "as is" value. This leaves you with a profit of between 5 percent to 15 percent of that value. Not bad for someone who never has to swing a hammer or raise a paintbrush.

A student of ours from Dayton, Ohio, got a call from a motivated seller who was responding to a flyer she put out on all the houses in her farm area. The seller was elderly and in poor health, and just couldn't take care of the property anymore. She was four months behind on her payments. Our student put the property under contract, then flipped the deal to another local investor for $4,500 profit.

When formulating how much to sell a terms deal to an investor, first calculate what you think the conservative net profit will be for this new investor. Then charge 10 percent to 20 percent of that long-term profit as your price to sell the deal.

Jerry, a retired General Motors employee in Michigan, did a mailing to expired listings (people who had listed their homes with a real estate agent but their property had not sold during the listing period). He found an owner who had inherited a house from his mother. Jerry agreed to buy the property for $20,000 with $2,000 cash to the seller, $1,900 of back payments, and subject to the seller's existing first mortgage. Then he sold the deal to another buyer and made $10,000 from it.

Here's another example of how easy this can be. We received an e-mail from Doug, an investor who lives in California. Doug found a motivated seller of a two-bedroom condo in Santa Barbara

---

FIGURE 7.2   Excerpt from Purchase Agreement with "Or Assigns" Preprinted
into the Agreement

John and Sally Homeowners, as Seller, and Home Buyers, LLC or assigns as
Buyer, hereby agree that the Seller shall sell and the Buyer shall buy the following described property UPON THE TERMS AND CONDITIONS HEREINAFTER SET
FORTH, which shall include the STANDARDS FOR REAL ESTATE TRANSACTIONS
set forth within this agreement.

---

who needed to quickly unload this property. Initially, the seller said
no to Doug's offer to buy the unit subject to the existing financing.
But one month later, he came back to Doug to take the deal. So Doug
called up a friend of his who lived in Chicago and had told Doug he
wanted to move to that area. His friend sent him a $6,000 cashier's
check the next day to buy out Doug's contract.

The Secret Clause That Allows You to Flip Your Deal

While any contract that doesn't specifically say it is "nonassignable" is legally assignable, you should make sure your purchase contract specifically says it is assignable. Simply sign up the deal with
your name, or better yet your company or LLC's name, "or assigns,"
as the Buyer. You can do this easily by preprinting the "or assigns"
into your purchase contract (see Figure 7.2) so you never forget to
include it.

If You're Still Wondering How You Can Sell a House You Don't Own

If you like the idea of making a quick cash profit but you're still
struggling with how you can sell a house you don't own to another
investor, you are not alone. Many of our students struggled with
that idea when they first got started. The key distinction is that you

are *not* selling the house; you are selling your *rights* under a contract to buy that house at a set price and terms.

This happens all the time in the real estate world. For example, a bank often sells a loan it originated to another party. It gets paid a fee to assign its rights under a promissory note and deed or trust/ mortgage to this other party. Or a tenant subleases a property to a subtenant. These are examples of selling a contractual right—in one case to receive payments from a loan and in the other to rent out the use of a property to a third party for a fee. Again, as long as no language in a contract exists that makes it nonassignable, all contracts are assignable.

The best part of assigning your interests in a contract to another party is that you don't need to be a licensed agent to do this. You are *not* representing a seller or helping people sell their house. You are acting as a principal, locking up a contract, and selling your interest in that contract for a profit. You don't need any kind of license to do this.

Take the case of Gary, a student who lives in San Diego. Gary called an old friend one day and found out his friend was in real trouble with a house he owned in Phoenix. Gary's friend owed $145,562 on a house only worth $130,000. So Gary got the second mortgage holder to accept a short sale of less than three cents on the dollar. He then turned and quickly sold the property to a retail cash buyer for $123,000. All totaled, Gary split the $26,000 profit he made 50-50 with his old friend. As you can imagine, both of them were thrilled.

Step Two: Find a Buyer for Your Deal

There are three sources of potential buyers for your deal:

- Retail buyers
- Other investors
- In-house "buyers' list"

A retail buyer is the average homebuyer who is looking to buy a house. "Retail" buyers might buy the house if you give them a good price. For example, you get a call from a seller responding to one of your postcards. This seller is two months away from losing his house to foreclosure. The house is worth about $250,000 in its current condition and, with about $5,000 worth of cosmetic work, it would sell for $275,000.

You meet with the seller and agree on a cash price of $180,000 with the closing date in 28 days. You find a buyer who'd like to own the house and is willing to pay as much as $220,000 to take the house in "as is" condition. Your buyer gets a house for $30,000 below its real market value and you make $40,000 (less your marketing costs and any share of closing costs you agree to pay). (See Figure 7.3.)

We'll go into more detail about how to handle this closing when we walk you through the final step of wholesaling a deal. For the moment, it's important to understand that selling the deal to a retail buyer will always make you more money than selling it to another investor. That makes sense because, in essence, you're cutting out the second middleman of the new investor. That's why you prefer to sell your deal to a retail buyer.

The second source of potential buyers is other investors. You want to find someone interested in paying you a cash assignment fee for the deal. In our current example, imagine you tried to find a retail buyer but weren't able to. But you did get an investor who was willing to pay $10,000 for the deal. You decide that $10,000 for the five hours' work you have tied into the deal is a decent hourly wage so you take it. (Later in this chapter, you'll learn how to find these investors—again, see Figure 7.3.)

The third source of buyers for your deal is the in-house "buyers' list" you've been cultivating. As both retail buyers and other investors call you about deals you have for sale, doesn't it make sense that if you don't have something they want at the moment, you add them to your buyers' list? Of course. Yet many investors forget to build

---

FIGURE 7.3   Selling to a Retail Buyer versus Another Investor

---

ARV	$275,000
"As is" value	$250,000
Your price	$180,000
Option One: Your Preferred Choice—Sell to a Retail Buyer	
Pays you	$220,000
Your price	($180,000)
Your costs	
closing	($ 2,000)
marketing	($ 1,000)
Your net profit	$ 37,000
Option Two: Your Second Choice—Sell to Another Investor	
You collect $10,000 "assignment" fee	
Your investor goes on to rehab and resell property	
ARV	$275,000
New investor's price	($190,000)
Repairs	($ 5,000)
Closing costs (twice)	($ 4,000)
Holding costs	($ 5,000)
Real estate commission (selling)	($ 16,500)
New investor's net profit	$ 54,500

---

these two important lists as they meet new prospective buyers. (Later in this chapter, we'll discuss the best ways to cultivate and use these two lists.)

The Biggest Secret to Flipping a Deal Fast

Most investors spend a few weeks looking for a retail buyer. If that doesn't work, then they contact their in-house investors list. If they still can't find a buyer, they get desperate and start advertising for other investors to buy the deal. Usually, these investors run out of time. Remember, the really good deals usually have a tight time crunch to make them work.

In our opinion, the real secret to flipping a deal fast is to look for all three types of buyers at the same time. Then you take the first decent offer to put *cash* in your hand. Simple as that.

Here's how this works in the real world. First, put your For Sale sign out in the front yard. Because it's hard to raise the price once your buyer sees it, this sign should advertise the property for sale to retail buyers. Investors won't mind that you're giving them a lower price. You can get this sign made for $30 to $60 at a local sign shop.

Also, flood the area with 30 to 40 handmade For Sale signs. These signs should be written with a fat black marker on sheets of poster board you've cut in half. After all, if you were looking for a bargain, would you rather see a fancy professional sign or a desperate handmade sign? Your buyers prefer the handmade signs too. They can almost smell the bargain they're going to get. (See Figure 7.4.) In fact, you'll probably get more investors calling from your signs than retail buyers.

You'll notice that we sent all our callers to our "24-hour recorded message." You'll likely get flooded with calls. Let technology help you screen them out by setting up voice mail to take these calls. (See *Making Big Money Investing in Real Estate,* pages 192–94, for detailed instructions on using a recorded message when marketing your properties.)

Three Little-Known Power Ad Secrets

In addition to using signs to market your property, tap into the power of classified ads to really get your phone ringing. Here are three little-known secrets to pumping up the response from all your classified advertising.

FIGURE 7.4   Sample Neighborhood Signs to Market Your Deal

Foreclosure!
3 Bed / 2 Bath
888-555-4567
24-hr. Rec. Msg.

Secret number one: Use an attention-grabbing headline on your ad. The first three to seven words need to be a headline that grabs the attention of your prospective buyer and locks their eyes onto your ad. Here are several possible attention grabbers to start your ad with if you want to find a buyer fast:

- Desperate Seller!
- Foreclosure!
- Forced Sale!
- Stranded Seller Must Sell in 7 Days or Less!
- Personal Circumstances Force Fast Sale!

Secret number two: Use attractive terms to sell your house fast. You'll learn more about selling with owner financing in the next chapter, but for the moment, read through the list of words that will attract a buyer's attention:

- Take over payments on my loan!
- Nonbank financing!
- No bank qualifying!
- 100% owner financing!
- Rent to own!

FIGURE 7.5   Sample Power Ads to Flip a Deal Fast

Foreclosure Pending. Need quick sale! 3 Bed/2 Bath. Will discount 10–15% below market if you can close fast. 619-555-4567 24-hr. msg.

Desperate, MUST SELL! 3 Bed/2 Bath House. Personal Circumstances Force Fast Sale. 877-555-4567 x 34. 24-hr. rec. msg.

Desperate Seller must sell in 14 days or lose house. Worth $311,850, will seriously consider any offer over $279,500 if you can close fast.

Secret number three: Use a low price to generate tons of calls. Your goal is to create an atmosphere of competition to bid up the price on the house. Be careful not to make an offer to prospective buyers that will force you to sell too cheaply.

Figure 7.5 shows several sample ads you can use to advertise your properties. Notice that some are directed at investors while others are for retail buyers.

Building Your In-House Buyers' List

As buyers respond to your marketing campaigns, make sure to always capture and save their contact information on your in-house buyers' list. Your goal is to build two unique lists that will allow you to turn your flipper deals faster and for more money than you ever could do by advertising for brand-new buyers each time you wholesale a deal.

The first list is your retail buyers' list, which includes all those people who have contacted you about buying one of your homes to live in themselves.

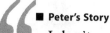

■ Peter's Story

I don't use any fancy software program to track my buyers' list. I simply keep all their contact information in a spreadsheet on my computer. Besides their names, phone numbers, and e-mail addresses, I also capture what type of home they are looking for and in what area. In addition, I capture the amount of down payment they have to work with, how much of a house they can qualify for a loan on, and how high of a monthly payment they can afford to pay. Then when I want to sell a house fast, I first go through my buyers' list, send out a quick e-mail to everyone, and call up those qualified for this specific house.   ■

The second list is your investors' list, which includes all the other investors you have met or who have called you about a prior deal you flipped. Again, keep track of their contact information, especially e-mail addresses. We love using e-mail to market a property to our investors' list because it's fast, effective, and *free*!

To build your list, go to your local real estate investors association monthly meetings. For a state-by-state list of what groups are active, contact the American Real Estate Investors Association Web site at <www.americanreia.com>. At your local association meeting, you'll be able to network with dozens of other investors who are looking for deals.

Second, get an e-mail address for every investor you can find and send an e-mail message like the one in Figure 7.6. This is your way of building your list of prospective investors. Beginning investors tend to forget to get the e-mail address of every investor who calls up about a deal. Don't lose out on the chance of building your investors' list; it's the fastest way to turn a deal for a quick cash profit.

FIGURE 7.6   Sample E-mail to Send to Prospective Investors to Survey Them

---

Subject: Investor Special

Hi there;

Thanks for e-mailing me about the investor special. This one is not available but I have been finding more properties lately than I am able to deal with due to my limited time.

I'll do my best to e-mail the details of any deals that I come across so that you can be one of the first to get a look at them. Because I negotiate my profits on the way into my deals, most properties I'll let you know about are 15 percent to 25 percent below market and some even come with creative financing in place.

If you can take a moment to answer the questions below, this will help me to determine what types of deal you are looking for. Occasionally, I'll find an absolute steal that needs some money to get the home quickly before anyone else gets it.

How much cash could you have at closing within 10 days (if you knew it was a great deal)?

$_____

Which of the following exit strategies have you used or are you comfortable with?

____ Fix and resell to retail buyer
____ Sell on rent-to-own to tenant-buyer
____ Hold as long-term rental
____ Sell with nonqualifying financing to nonconforming buyers

How many deals have you done? _____

How do you calculate a "good deal"? (Please be specific, i.e., percent of after-repair value, or you must make at least $10,000, etc.)

_____

_____

FIGURE 7.6   Sample E-mail to Send to Prospective Investors to Survey Them (Continued)

Lowest price homes you'd consider: $_____

Highest price homes you'd consider: $_____

Preferred AFTER-REPAIR price range: $_____

Areas you prefer to invest in: _____

Areas you will NOT invest in: _____

Which types of repair work are you comfortable with?_____

_____

Your Name: _____

Address: _____

Best Day Phone: _____

Other Phone # to try: _____

Fax: _____

E-mail: _____

If you prefer, you can print this form and fax it to me at 619-555-1234 or just hit reply and put your answers in the appropriate places.

Thanks,

Brenda Investor
619-555-1256

P.S. I know that I asked a lot of questions. It's just that I want to know exactly what deals I should send your way to save you time. By taking five minutes now to share your criteria for a deal that makes you money, you will save hours in looking for new deals. You can leverage your time by letting me be one of your bird dogs spotting potential deals for you. I make an assignment fee and you go on to even bigger profits, and everyone wins!

P.P.S.
From time to time I'll be sending you e-mails that list new potential deals for you to consider. These e-mails will say, "Bargain Finder Report" in the subject line. Have a great day!

Step Three: Close with Your Buyer

Once you find a buyer who wants to buy your deal, you'll need to set up a closing with this person. A closing is a fancy name for a time to sit down and sign all the final paperwork that assigns your interest in the deal to this new buyer and for you to collect your check from your new buyer.

If you're flipping the deal to another investor, this closing is fast and easy. Simply get this investor to bring you a cashier's check for the amount of your assignment fee. Collect this check first, then sign an Assignment of Real Estate Contract form (see Figure 7.7). Give this buyer all your original contract paperwork with the seller and you've completed the deal.

■ **Peter's Story**

I feel it's important that I make sure the person I sell a deal to really can perform on his end with the seller. While I'm *technically* done with the deal once I assign it over to my buyer, I still stay in contact with the seller to make sure he or she gets treated the right way from this new buyer. I know I don't have to do this; it's just that I feel it's the right way to do business.   ■

If you are selling your deal to a retail buyer, you sometimes have to do more work to make the closing happen. If you are selling a terms deal in which your new buyer wants to buy the property to live in because of the easy financing the deal has in place, then this closing with your buyer is easy. For example, take our $250,000 house that needs $5,000 in repairs to be worth $275,000. You agreed with the seller to buy the property for $5,000 down and take over subject to the seller's $240,000 mortgage.

In this example, your retail buyer agrees to pay you $265,000 for the house in "as is" condition because you're letting the buyer get in with this existing financing in place. Your new buyer agrees

FIGURE 7.7   Sample Assignment of Real Estate Contract Form

Assignment of Real Estate Contract

FOR VALUE RECEIVED, the undersigned wholesaler (Assignor) hereby assigns, transfers, and sets over to _____ (Assignee) all rights, title, and interest held by the Assignor in and to the following described contract:

The Assignee hereby assumes and agrees to perform all the remaining and executory obligations of the Assignor under the Contract in good faith and within the time periods established by said Contract. Assignee agrees to indemnify and hold the Assignor harmless from any claim or demand resulting from nonperformance by the Assignee. The Assignee hereby commits $_____ in certified funds as a nonrefundable deposit and will pay an additional compensation in the amount of $_____ prior to closing on the Contract. In the event that Assignee defaults on the Contract, then the nonrefundable deposit mentioned herein shall be retained as complete liquidated damages by Assignor and all rights to the above Contract will revert back to Assignor.

The Assignee agrees to defend, indemnify, and hold Assignor harmless for any deficiency or defect in the legality or enforceability of the terms of said Contract.

The Assignee agrees and understands that the Assignor is not acting as a real estate agent or broker, but rather the Assignor is a principal in the transaction who is selling their interest in the above-referenced Contract to Assignee.

This assignment shall be binding upon and inure to the benefit of the parties, their successors and assigns.

This agreement is subject to the following conditions:

_____

_____

_____

Date of this agreement: _____

_____   _____
Wholesaler / Assignor   Assignee

to give you $25,000 cash, of which you give $5,000 to the seller and keep the other $20,000 as your profit. Your new buyer now gets title to the house and agrees to take over the monthly payments. (You'll learn more about this type of deal in the next chapter.)

You could also have had your new buyer give you $20,000 and then assign him your contract with the seller. This would also work. (We'll go into the details of why we prefer the first way over assigning the deal to the new buyer in the next chapter.)

Why is flipping a cash deal to a retail buyer more work? Usually the retail buyer will use a conventional loan to fund part or all of the purchase of the property, and whenever a conventional lender is involved, things become more complicated simply because this lender has all its own rules and requirements for doing things. But it's worth the extra effort—you'll make more money when you sell a deal to a retail buyer rather than to an investor.

Besides just getting a cash fee to assign your contract to a buyer, there are two more ways to accomplish your flip to a retail buyer when a conventional lender is involved. We aren't complicating this to impress you. It's just that when we started flipping deals in the various states we buy properties in, we soon learned that the textbook way of closing these deals didn't always work when conventional lenders were added to the equation. So you're about to learn the lessons of years of trial and error to find the winning formulas.

Imagine you have a house worth $325,000 in "as is" condition. The seller is five weeks away from losing the sale to the foreclosure auction. He owes $210,000 against the property and is $20,000 behind in payments. The house needs about $15,000 worth of cosmetic repairs to show well and be able to sell for its ARV of $375,000. Because you didn't want to do the rehab work, you negotiated the best cash price you could with the seller, knowing you would flip the deal to someone else. After using all the negotiating ideas learned from this book (plus a few others you've picked up over the years), you got the seller to agree on a price of $275,000.

You turn around and find a couple who want to buy the house in its "as is" condition for $315,000. They figure they're getting a great deal and they're actually looking forward to fixing it up the way they want before they move in. And you're thrilled because you'll make $40,000 on this deal.

Now let's look at the two ways you can close this deal and get paid your $40,000.

First, you can do a "simultaneous closing." This means you close on the deal with your buyer and seller at the same time, using your buyer's money to pay the seller his $275,000, of which $230,000 goes to pay off the first mortgage and $45,000 goes to the seller less his share of the closing costs. Your title or escrow company (whoever is doing the closing for you) sets up a double closing. You and the seller meet in one conference room and sign all the documents needed to complete the transaction with the seller. Then you walk down the hall into the separate closing room with your buyers and collect their money and deed the house over to them. Then the escrow agent takes the money the buyers' lender paid to pay off the existing lender, to pay the seller his money, and to give you your $40,000 check. This is the easiest way to do the closing whenever you can. The key is that the buyer's lender will have to be open to funding the deal that involves a double closing. This works 30 percent to 50 percent of the time, depending on where you live.

The second way to handle the closing is a fallback if the lender won't let you do a simultaneous closing. You can take this three-party transaction—you, the seller, and your buyer—and turn it into a two-party transaction. Because the buyer is the one with all the money, you can't get rid of him. But you can temporarily get rid of the seller by having her deed you the property subject to the existing loan. Now that you are on title, the buyer's lender will be satisfied and you can close directly with your new buyers. You simply agree on paper with your seller that the escrow instructions will order the escrow agent to use the new buyer's funds to pay off the existing loan, to then give the seller his share of the proceeds, and finally to give what's left to you, the investor.

Again, we know this looks like a hassle, and it is. But in the real world of investing, sometimes the textbook moves like "simultaneous closings" don't work and you need a street-smart backup. That's why we shared this fallback strategy with you to get the deal to close.

■ **Peter's Story**

It can sometimes be a total hassle to deal with a buyer's lender to make a deal work. Just keep reminding yourself that, for your effort, you're going to collect a fat check in the end. Keep saying it over and over to yourself—there's a fat check at the end of this for me . . . there's a fat check at the end of this for me . . .   ■

■ **David's Story**

Be careful that you don't get caught on the treadmill of flipping deals. Yes, you can make some exciting money by flipping properties, but when you stop working, your income stops flowing. If you need quick cash, then flip deals to create that cash flow. But also develop the resources to be able to build a portfolio of properties for your long-term financial freedom. I look at flipping deals as a way to make money from deals that I wouldn't want to have to do all the rehab work on or deal with over time. You can ignore this advice if you want and flip all the deals you sign up. You'll make lots of money. I just want you to have more than money. I want you to have the freedom to be wealthy and the security to enjoy your future without having to race around hunting up your next deal. This means passive income, and this means building a portfolio of investment properties to hold over time.   ■

Investing for Long-Term Wealth Buildup

One of the decisions you are going to have to make in your investing business is whether you are going to invest for short-term cash flow or long-term wealth buildup or some hybrid of the two.

You have already learned how to turn your foreclosure deal into fast cash, so it's time to turn our attention to ways to structuring your properties for long-term equity buildup. Both are important. You need cash flow to have spendable income to support your family, but you need long-term equity growth to build the lifestyle and future you want for yourself.

■ **David's Story**

At our workshops, one of the most common questions is, "What do I wish I would have known when I got started investing that would have had the most dramatic positive impact on my success?" It's a great question that cuts straight past all the hype to the core of what's essential. Here is my answer: I wish I had held on to more of the properties I bought. I look at the houses I turned in the early days of my investing after only owning or controlling them for 12 months or less and I think, If only I still had those properties . . .

In my first year alone, if I still owned or controlled all the houses I had under contract, I would be about $3,000,000 wealthier! And this is a very conservative estimate.   ■

The exit strategies you choose must meet the needs of your own situation. You may need to turn a quick cash profit like you need your next breath of air. Fair enough. If that's the case, use the ideas in Chapter 7 to turn your properties for fast cash. Just make sure to hold on to some of the properties you're buying for your future well-being. You don't want to get trapped in the rat race, always looking for the next deal to flip, and the next, and the next.

You may already have solid income, whether from a business, a job, or other investments. Great. In that case, you'll want to rely on the exit strategies described in this chapter to maximize your long-term wealth buildup. The best part of purchase option investing is that you control how much you make and when you make it.

Strategy #1: Rent Out the Property

While this book isn't about being a landlord, you should understand that this traditional way of holding on to properties over time has worked for thousands of investors. It's not our preferred niche of investing, but we still use it as an exit strategy for a portion of our real estate portfolio. Just be aware that being a landlord can be a drag at times.

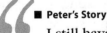

■ Peter's Story

I still have about 30 traditional rentals going. They provide good cash flow and allow me to hang on to the properties over the long haul. The biggest downside is that traditional rentals are time-intensive. In the past, I handled this by forming my own property management company. But this still took so much energy away from my family and other investing activities. That's what led me to search out a better way to handle my growing portfolio. Today, the majority of my portfolio is structured on a rent-to-own basis.   ■

Strategy #2: Sell Properties on a Rent-to-Own Basis

One of our favorite exit strategies is to sell a property on a rent-to-own basis. Because you're putting someone with an owner's mentality (as opposed to a renter's mind-set) into the home, your property will likely be better cared for. And because you'll collect a hefty nonrefundable option fee up front that's 3 percent to 5 percent of the value of the property, you're in a strong position to collect your rent each month from your tenant-buyer.

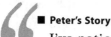

■ Peter's Story

I've noticed that only one out of four or five tenant-buyers actually takes the next step and exercises an option to buy. In my opinion, this makes offering your property on a rent-to-own basis a great holding strategy and turns your properties into hands-off rentals. I recommend pushing most or all of the day-to-day maintenance onto your tenant-buyer's shoulders. This, more than anything else, has helped me escape the landlord trap of tenants and toilets. Today I spend less time managing my real estate portfolio than I did when I had my own in-house property management company, which I sold off several years ago.   ■

For complete details on how to successfully price, advertise, and sell properties on a rent-to-own basis, see *Making Big Money Investing in Real Estate,* pages 181–229.

Strategy #3: Sell with "Owner Financing"

Considering that in many areas of the country, 75 percent or more of renters cannot qualify to purchase the median-priced house in that area with conventional financing, you probably don't need any convincing about the appeal nonbank financing has to the appetites of a huge percentage of would-be homebuyers.

Many potential buyers have credit problems or not enough income to qualify for traditional financing, so you'll find that when you offer one of your properties with owner financing, you'll get swamped with people who want to buy.

Owner financing simply means that you, the seller of a property, act as the bank. You finance the sale so your buyer doesn't have to go to a conventional lender and qualify for a traditional loan.

Most beginning investors see owner financing as an option only for properties they own free and clear. For example, suppose you have a house you own free and clear worth $400,000. You sell it to a buyer for a down payment of $40,000 (10 percent) and carry back the other $360,000 as a mortgage to be paid to you over the next five years. This is the best-known form of owner financing, where a seller acts like the bank on a property he owns free and clear. But as a savvy investor, you can tap into the power of owner financing in many more powerful ways.

■ **David's Story**

Remember talking about buying properties subject to the existing financing? You might not have realized it but that's a form of owner financing. For example, say you found a seller of a $275,000 house who was four months behind in his payments. You agreed to buy that house by making up the seller's back payments and taking title subject to the existing $245,000 loan. The seller solves his problem, which is the looming foreclosure, and you get a house for about $6,500 in back payments with about $20,000 to $25,000 of equity. In essence, this was an owner-financed deal because you used the seller's existing loan as a way of leveraging yourself into the property.   ■

You can use this same concept when you sell a property by selling it subject to the existing financing. Continuing on with the previous example, you now have the house under contract but you don't have the $8,000 you need to catch up the back payments and pay for closing costs. So you decide to sell the house with owner financing and let your new buyer give you the funds needed to bring the payments current. You advertise using techniques described later in this chapter and find a buyer who agrees to purchase the house for $290,000 with 10 percent down and you carry back the balance. So now you collect $29,000 as a down payment, then use $8,000 to make up the back payments and pay for closing costs. You've just made $21,000 cash up front plus you'll make another $8,000 on the back end (see Figure 8.1). And there are two more hidden profit centers we haven't even shared with you yet.

■ **David's Story**

Look at your local Sunday paper. In many cities, more than 200 properties are offered for sale at any given time. Yet out of these 200, less than 20 will be offered with no bank financing. That means that you are offering something that's scarce. Combine this with the fact that the average renter can't qualify to buy the median-priced home in most cities and you recognize that not only is the *supply* limited but the *demand* is greater for an owner-financed house than for a traditionally financed one. I may not know much about economics, but even I know that when supply is limited and demand increases, prices must go up.

When I sell with owner financing, I typically get 5 percent to 10 percent above market value for the property—and without any real estate commission—simply because the financing has made the

---

FIGURE 8.1   Sample Owner-Carry Deal

Value	$275,000
Your price	$253,000
Existing first mortgage you took title subject to	$245,000
Your CASH costs up front	
Back payments	$ 6,500
Closing costs	$ 1,500
Your selling price	$290,000
Your purchase price	($253,000)
Your profit	$37,000
Form of your profits	
Cash	
Buyer's down payment	$ 29,000
Cash YOU put in deal	($ 8,000)
Net cash up front	$ 21,000
Note you carry for your buyer	$ 8,000

(Note: You'll also earn interest from the note you carry back for your buyer.)

house more valuable! After all, your buyers are not really buying the house; they're buying the financing. Now, I don't get all this money up front, but I like creating a hands-off income stream that has a future payoff.   ■

Six Benefits to the Buyer for Using Owner Financing

1. *Fast closing.* You can close in as little as 72 hours. Just try that with a conventional lender!
2. *Easy monthly payments.* You're in control of structuring the payments. If you want, you can even charge them "interest-only" payments, which lowers their monthly payment.
3. *No banks to deal with.* This means no bureaucracy and red tape and loan committees to work through.

4. *Almost no paperwork to fill out.* Yes, you'll get a loan application from your buyers, but they'll save hours not having to fill out redundant bank forms and creating fancy loan application packets.

5. *Doesn't matter what their credit or income is like.* Depending on the amount of down payment buyers have to work with and the amount they can afford to pay you each month, you can work with buyers no matter what their credit is like.

6. *Flexible terms on the financing.* You can structure the financing to meet your buyer's needs. If your buyer needs two years to clean up his credit and then refinance, you can set up the financing to have a balloon note due for the outstanding balance after two or three years. *You* are the one in control of structuring the financing.

Selling with owner financing is not the right fit for every situation, but it's a useful tool to have in your toolbox. Here are three reasons that might make selling one of your properties with owner financing the right exit strategy for you:

1. *You need a large amount of money up front.* Typically, you'll be able to collect 10 percent to 15 percent as a down payment. This can often be your source of funding to get into the deal. Or if you need money up front to live on, owner financing allows you to satisfy your immediate cash needs while still creating a passive income stream and back-end profit.

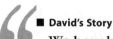

■ **David's Story**

We bought a house in southern California with two of our Mentorship students, Mark and Trish. We bought the house subject to the existing financing. When we were planning our exit strategy, Mark and Trish said they wanted to get as much money up front from the sale as possible. We decided to sell the house with owner financing and got $25,000 of our total $28,000 profit up front within 60 days. ■

2. *You need to get a higher-than-market rent payment.* Because your buyer will get to write off the interest paid on the property, you can charge a significantly higher-than-market monthly rent payment and still save your buyer money over conventional financing.

■ **Peter's Story**

I was helping one of our Mentorship students structure a deal in Ohio. She had purchased a property from a seller who was in preforeclosure but the monthly payment was $200 over the market rent for the house. I explained to her that by selling with owner financing, she could find a buyer willing to pay that much, which in this case was $1,100 a month. She did, in fact, find a buyer who paid her the $1,100 by selling the property on an installment land contract—a form of owner financing. ■

3. *You want to make sure you will have no more responsibility with the property.* Even selling on a rent-to-own basis can require some property management on your part. By selling with owner financing, you truly do step into the hands-off role of passive institutional investor. Your buyer is legally responsible for everything involving the property, including making her payment to you each month. Also, because you're getting three to four times the up-front money than if you were selling on a rent-to-own basis, you can be much more secure knowing your buyer will take care of the property and live up to her side of the deal, including paying the monthly payments on time.

Take care that when you choose to sell a property with owner financing, you take steps to protect yourself. You'll learn about wraparound mortgages and land contracts soon, both of which are used to protect yourself when you are selling with owner financing. One of the best protections you can have is to have definite criteria when you should *not* sell with owner financing.

Here are the three criteria when you *shouldn't* sell with owner financing:

1. *When your buyer doesn't have at least 10 percent to pay as a down payment.* If he has less than this amount, don't sell him the property with owner financing. You can sell it to him on a rent-to-own basis and agree that if he pays you at least 10 percent down by a specific date, you will give him the option of having you carry back the financing. You should not give someone title to your property, be it legal title or equitable title, who hasn't paid you at least 10 percent down.

2. *When your buyer wants to buy with none of her own money.* While we love buying without any of our own money, rarely will we allow anyone to buy a property from us where we agree to help finance this new buyer but he has no money of his own at stake. Why? We know, just like lenders know, that when a buyer has her own money at risk she is much more likely to live up to the terms and conditions of the loan.

3. *When you aren't getting enough profit in the deal to make it worthwhile.* We like to realize enough profit out of the deal up front so that if worst came to worst and our buyer defaulted, even if we never saw another penny from that deal, we would still feel we had a victory. Obviously, if your buyer defaults, you will move to get your money, oftentimes by foreclosing. Still, you can protect your peace of mind by

always knowing you made enough that you are comfortable saying, "Next."

Once you've decided to sell with owner financing, you need to know how to protect yourself. To do this, you are going to use a few simple tools. The first tool you'll use is a wraparound mortgage or All-Inclusive Trust Deed (AITD). As you learned in Chapter 2, a mortgage and a deed of trust are security instruments that ensure a borrower lives up to all the terms and conditions of a loan. The borrower signs a promissory note, which is evidence of the debt, and either a mortgage or deed of trust to secure the debt depending on which state the property is located in. A wraparound mortgage or AITD is a specialized version of an ordinary mortgage or deed of trust. We will go into more detail soon, but first remember when you learned about buying property subject to the existing financing how you can just take over making the payments on the loan. Just like you can buy subject to the existing financing, you can also sell subject to the existing financing. If you do this, you want to protect yourself if your buyer does not live up to the terms and conditions of the underlying loan and mortgage or deed of trust. You want to make sure your buyer maintains the property, keeps the property insured, pays the taxes, and makes the monthly payments on time.

If you just sold the property subject to the existing financing without using the techniques in this section, you'd be powerless to stop your buyer from defaulting on the terms of the loan. You would no longer have any stake or say in the matter. To give yourself the power to force your buyer to comply, use a document called a wraparound mortgage or AITD. This is an additional document by which you can legally obligate your buyer to honor all the terms and conditions of the existing financing. In essence, it says that the buyer agrees to live up to all the terms and conditions of the existing financing, plus the buyer will pay back to you any money you carried back from the buyer's purchase of the property from you.

For example, imagine you bought a house for $300,000 with $10,000 down and subject to an existing $290,000 first mortgage. You decide to sell that house on a wraparound mortgage. The house is worth $330,000 to a cash buyer, but you know that if you offer nonbank financing it's worth more. You find a buyer who's willing to buy from you for $350,000 with $35,000 down. To protect yourself, you get your buyer to sign a wraparound mortgage (if you live in a deed of trust state, then you would have the buyer sign an AITD, which acts just like a wraparound mortgage), securing that the buyer will not only pay you the rest of the money owed, but will also live up to the terms and conditions of the first mortgage.

Many investors will have the buyer pay them one payment each month and they will pay a portion of that payment to cover the existing first mortgage payment. In our previous example, if your buyer agreed to pay you interest-only payments at 9 percent on the $315,000 that you carried back, you would collect $2,362.50 each month from your buyer. With this money, you'd be obligated to pay the mortgage payment on the first mortgage of $2,000 a month. The extra $362.50 is yours to keep as one of your profit centers.

You could have your buyer pay the $2,000 directly to the first mortgage lender and then send you a second check for $362.50 each month, but we don't recommend it. While it's more work to collect the larger check and send the $2,000 to the existing first mortgage lender, you know your buyer is paying that mortgage on time. We suggest you collect the full payment of $2,362.50 and use that money to pay the first mortgage. If your buyer doesn't pay one month, then you won't pay the first mortgage and you will immediately get a local attorney or foreclosure service to start the foreclosure. You can be nice and work with the buyer on the phone to find a solution. But any solution you work toward will have the deadline of the ticking foreclosure clock. Explain that it's not your decision to do it this way; it's your partner's choice. You're the "good cop" trying to find a way out, but you can't stop the "bad cop" (your partner) from moving forward with the foreclosure unless you receive payment of what is owed.

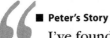

Peter's Story

I've found the best way to protect myself is to always start an eviction or foreclosure as soon as my renter or buyer has defaulted. While I'm empathetic and nice, I don't stop until I either get the property back or I get payment in full. I guarantee you'll hear a million stories if you allow excuses. I urge you to set this firm policy, explain it to your renters and buyers up front, then hold them accountable to this specific standard. Anytime I have deviated from this in the past, I've regretted it.   ■

Using Land Contracts

A land contract (also known as a "bond for deed" or "agreement for deed," or "contract for deed") is another way to protect yourself when you sell with owner financing. A land contract is an installment sale by which you sell a property to a buyer who gets equitable title and you keep legal title. What's the difference? Not much. Equitable title means the buyer owns the property and gets to live in the house, write off all the deductions on tax forms, sell the property, etc. The buyer just isn't named on *legal title* (i.e., having the property *deeded* to them.)

Think about it this way. When you buy a car from a dealer and the dealer finances the sale, you get to drive the car off the lot (equitable title). But the dealer's name is on the *pink slip* (legal title). When you pay off the entire loan, the dealer signs over the pink slip to you. If you default on the loan, the dealer takes back the car.

A land contract is essentially like a wraparound mortgage or AITD except that, in several states, it's easier to get the property back in the event your buyer defaults than if you sold the property on a wraparound mortgage or AITD. For example, in Ohio if your buyer has less than 10 percent equity in a property and defaults on the terms of the land contract, you can actually evict him from the property. This process takes a few weeks. If you sold the property on a wraparound mortgage, it could take you months to go through Ohio's judicial foreclosure process.

In some states, however, selling on a land contract is a bad idea because of the difficulties posed to the seller trying to foreclose on a defaulting buyer. In California, for example, if you sold on a land contract, you would have to start a "quiet title action" lawsuit to extinguish your buyer's ownership interest before you could take the next step and evict her from the property. You are much better off in California selling on an AITD.

Ask a *good* real estate attorney how land contracts versus wraparound mortgages or AITDs measure up in your state. The real key will be which way it's easier for you to get the property back or force the sale of the property if your buyer defaults. Ask your attorney the legal process you would need to follow if your buyer defaults. Then compare this process to the one you would need to go through if you sold the house on a wraparound mortgage or AITD.

The bottom line is: If you ever sell with owner financing subject to the existing financing, *always* use either a wraparound mortgage or AITD or a land contract to protect your interest.

■ Peter's Story

Recently an e-mail was forwarded to me about how one of our students in Colorado, Larry, just sold a house on an installment land contract. Larry's wife found a seller who was three payments behind on his mortgage. Larry bought the house for $226,000, subject to the existing financing. He quickly refinanced the house to drop his payment to $1,405 PITI. He then put an ad in the paper and found a couple who wanted to buy the house from him for $250,000. They gave him $10,000 down, plus will pay him $2,066 each month. This gives Larry $661 a month of hassle-free income. ■

Selling with Owner Financing—Step-by-Step

Step One: Marketing the Property

Let's say you have decided to sell your investment property with owner financing. Your first step is to market the property and generate as many prospective buyers as possible.

■ **David's Story**

In my opinion, the single most important factor in selling a house fast is to create intense competition for the property. Most investors struggle with this. They are slow to market the property. There is power behind the urgency you create when selling a house. The first two weeks it's on the market are critical. I'm a big believer in group showings with as many people as I can get to the property at the same time. This means I don't try to overqualify or sell the house over the phone. Instead, I push everyone who's remotely interested in the property to come to see the house at the same time. I love the way buyers behave so nicely and decide so quickly when they fear losing the house to another family at the showing.   ■

Besides placing signs, running ads in your local paper's real estate classified "For Sale" section is the best way to find a buyer for your property. Building on the classified advertising techniques you learned in the last chapter, Figure 8.2 offers three power ads you can use as templates when you're selling a property with owner financing.

Notice that each of these ads almost ignores the property and instead sells the financing. This is the same technique that car dealerships use when they advertise. They don't focus on the price; instead, they emphasize the payment and the amount of money needed up front.

FIGURE 8.2   Power Ads When Selling a House with Owner Financing

---

> **EZ Qualifying! OWC. Must sell now! Price Reduced for Quick Sale. 3br/2ba, dbl gar. 619-555-1234.**

Or

> **Desperate, Must Sell! $25,000 down take over pymts. on my loan. No banks to deal with. 4br./ 3ba. 888-444-1212. 24-hr. rec. msg.**

Or

> **Nonbank Financing! Bad Credit OK! Small down payment with owner to carry entire balance! 3br./ 2.5ba. house. Details call 888-444-1212 ext. 44. 24-hr. rec. msg.**

You might be wondering where the price is in these ads. We recommend you *don't* include the price. Instead, use your ad to drive as many prospective buyers as possible to your recorded voice-mail message. (How to create an effective voice-mail message was covered in Chapter 4.) Just as the purpose of your classified ad is to generate the phone call, the purpose of your voice-mail message is to get a caller to communicate his contact information and the monthly payment range and down payment he has to work with.

Sample Voice-Mail Script for Selling with Owner Financing

Hello and thanks for calling. This is your chance to quickly and easily own your dream home. Right now we have a beautiful 4-bedroom, 2½-bath home in Briargate. This home has a stunning view of the mountains, and a great yard with a deck; it's very close to shopping and is on a quiet cul-de-sac.

We're offering this home with long-term owner financing. There are no banks to deal with and no long forms to fill out! This is the simplest and easiest way for you to own your own home.

To help us help you, after the tone, leave your name and telephone number, along with the range you want to keep your monthly payments in, and the amount of down payment you have to work with. Obviously, the larger the monthly payments you can handle and the larger the down payment you have to work with, the easier it will be for us to choose you to buy this house.

Thanks for calling and remember to leave your name, telephone number, monthly payment, and down payment you have to work with, and if it's a match, we'll call you back as soon as we're back in the office.

Signs—Your Most Effective Source of Buyers

Whether you're selling the house on a rent-to-own basis or with owner financing, signs are one of the most important ways to attract qualified buyers to the property. Again, as recommended in the previous chapter, use a combination of two professional-looking signs in the front yard and the corner lot along with plain handwritten signs on simple poster board or corrugated plastic sheets. (See Figure 8.3.)

FIGURE 8.3   Sample Neighborhood Sign to Sell with Owner Financing

No Bank Qualifying!
100% Owner Carry!
4bd./2ba. House
888-222-8488 ext. 45
24-hr. Rec. Msg.

■ **Student's Story**

I received a deposit and a promise of $8,000 in option money from a couple who saw one of my bandit signs (the first sign that I ever put out, as a matter of fact). The man said he was driving to Lowe's when he caught sight of a tired-looking little yellow sign on a stake by the side of the road. The sign was curled up and flopped over so all he could read was "rent" and "3 bed." He said he got out of his car, went over to the sign, and held up the corners so he could read the whole thing. He got out his cell phone and punched in the toll-free number right there. So, I guess these signs really do attract the attention of people in the market for a new place!—Heidi, Alaska.   ■

When you're using signs in a city or area that doesn't allow signs, try putting your signs out Friday afternoon before everyone is driving home from work or very early on Saturday morning. If you remove them by Sunday night, you'll usually be able to avoid those people who don't like your signs as much as you do. In some areas, using your own wooden stakes or metal sign holders seems to relax the officials. One added benefit of handmade signs on poster board is that city authorities tend to see them as one-time events from harmless homeowners, not products of huge real estate investment firms (if only they knew, right!).

Your local city probably does have rules about the use, or even against the use, of these signs. Because of that, we're not telling you to use signs; we're merely sharing that other investors have used signs to make a lot of money. You'll have to make your own autonomous decision after talking with your attorney, CPA, insurance agent, and psychologist. (How's that for a disclaimer?)

Flyers—Your Ace in the Hole

One powerful guerrilla marketing technique to generate leads on prospective buyers is using flyers advertising the property for sale. You can deliver these flyers to homes in the surrounding neighborhood. (See Figure 8.4.) Don't forget to look for other places to post flyers such as grocery stores, major employers, community bulletin boards, your local coffeehouse, etc.

■ Peter's Story

I recommend you hire someone else to put out these flyers for you. If you really want to be successful as an investor, you need to understand the real value of your time. It's hard to earn $50 an hour, let alone $500 or more an hour, if you're doing activities you could pay someone else $10 to $15 an hour to do.   ■

FIGURE 8.4   Sample Flyer to Find Buyers

$500 Reward

Wanted: The Perfect Neighbor

We want you to have the perfect neighbor, so you can help us to choose your neighbor!

That's right . . . if you can help us to find a great person or family to move into this:

3-bedroom, 2-bath home at 345 Vista View Way

We'll pay you a "reward" of $500

It's available as:
Rent to own
Owner Carry Financing
Nonqualifying Financing

Call 866-555-1234. 24-hr. rec. msg.
or office 303-555-1234

www.RentToOwnDenver.com

Setting Up a Realistic Marketing Timeline

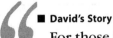

■ David's Story

For those number crunchers who want the metrics, here's a snapshot of the numbers I see when I'm marketing my properties. I get a huge number of signs (40 to 60) out the first two weeks. I put them out immediately and replenish them early on Friday afternoon. (Actually, I hire someone to post them.) This gets me about 25 calls on average. Of these, six to eight potential buyers will show up to see the property.

Signs are critical to find buyers even with the calls your classified ads generate. Typically, I receive 30 to 40 calls from my ads over two weeks, of which eight to ten people will come see the property. This means I get 14 to 18 prospective buyers to see the property within the first three weeks I have it on the market.

I place a *big* emphasis on showing a house to large groups (even if only one or two of the people really are qualified). Normally it takes me two to four showings to fill a property and I collect nonrefundable deposits to hold from an average of .75 people who don't end up buying in addition to the one deposit to hold I get from the person who does buy.

The key is to push hard to generate traffic through the house for the first two weeks. If I get busy and slow down, I lose momentum, which I feel is *critical* to selling a house. Prospective buyers do pick up on this. On these occasions, it takes me about four to six weeks on average to sell to a tenant-buyer (rent to own) or buyer (owner financing).　■

Two More Hidden Profit Centers in Your Owner-Financing Deals

Because most of the buyers you'll find for your owner-financing properties have poor credit, they'll be more than willing to pay an above-market interest rate if you provide them with the financing. Most of your financing will be at 6 percent to 8 percent, and you'll be able to charge your buyer 8.9 percent to 10.9 percent interest. This will leave you with a healthy spread in the interest rates.

For example, let's say you bought a house subject to its existing $200,000 first mortgage at an interest rate of 7 percent. Then you sell the house on a wraparound mortgage for $230,000 with a $30,000 down payment and an interest rate of 8.9 percent. Not only did you make your $30,000 from the down payment, but you now have a spread in the interest rates that earns you 1.9 percent on the entire $200,000 balance. That passive income flows to you each month.

Finally, depending on the underlying loan and the financing you structure for your buyer, you may have one more profit center—the spread in the amortization of the loans. Referring to the previous example, let's say the loan you took title subject to is paying down $150 each month (and the amount keeps growing). But the loan you made to your buyer is interest only. That means each month, the underlying loan is getting paid off and down the road will be much lower than $200,000. For example, in five years your buyer may refinance the loan you made him of $200,000. At that point, the underlying loan may have paid down to $192,000. This means you make an extra $8,000 payday.

Six Things Top Investors Do to Sell Fast

1. They stay in control during all phone conversations to set appointments. Successful investors firmly take charge right from the start.
2. They know how to *pack* a showing with five to ten families or potential buyers. Remember, more is better.
3. They *love* collecting deposits and feel great about people giving them money. Being comfortable accepting money isn't something you can just take for granted. It's a state of mind that can be cultivated over time.
4. They know it only takes one person to buy the property and they feel confident that if the monthly payment and up-front money are right and the house looks decent, they *will* find a buyer.
5. They *expect* to collect a deposit to hold the property on the spot. Real buyers put up or shut up. A promise from a buyer only means something if it's accompanied with cash.
6. They don't care if they find the *perfect* buyer at the absolute *top* monthly payment and price. They just want a *good* buyer who gives them money right away.

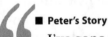

■ **Peter's Story**

I've gone through all the "Oh my gosh, am I really going to be able to find someone . . . Oh poor me, what if I can't . . . what if I have to make the payments for the next six months myself . . . or if the seller freaks out . . . Did I really buy this right. . . ." Provided you've done your homework and bought right, have faith you will find a buyer. That confidence is contagious to buyers. Keep saying to yourself over and over, like a mantra, "I'm only looking for one buyer." ■

A Powerful Selling Strategy: Rent-to-Own into Owner-Carry Financing

One useful strategy is to combine selling a house on a rent-to-own basis with owner-carry financing. For example, we sold a four-bedroom house for $279,980 on a two-year rent-to-own basis. Our tenant-buyers paid us a $15,000 option payment and a monthly rent of $1,695. At the end of the two years, they still couldn't qualify to buy using conventional financing, but they really wanted the house. So we agreed to finance them ourselves by selling it to them on an AITD (the house was in California where this is the best way to protect yourself when selling subject to the existing financing). We bumped their price to $285,000 and they gave us $15,000 more money as a down payment. We charged them interest-only payments at 8.9 percent, which meant they paid $1,891.25 a month. We also set a deadline for them to refinance the property within two years of the sale, when a balloon note for the rest of the money came due.

If you choose this combined selling strategy, here are your benefits:

- *Less risk.* You only rent-to-own first and don't agree to the owner-carry financing until after the buyer has proven to be a good risk.
- *Lots of control for you.* You don't obligate yourself to sell with owner financing; you merely agree to talk it through toward the end of the rent-to-own option period.
- *Growing streams of monthly cash flow.* You'll get a lot more money each month from your buyers than the rent they used to pay. Because, at this point, they are owners, they also get to write off the interest they pay on their taxes. This means the net cost to your buyer will usually be negligible.
- *You sell at the future price.* When you sell on a rent-to-own basis, you charge an inflated price. When you roll this rent-

to-own property into owner-carry financing, you can again bump the price because this nonbank financing commands a premium in the marketplace.

- *It's easy to find people who want to buy a house like this.* There are many times more buyers for rent-to-own or owner-financed homes than for traditional properties.
- *You save thousands in real estate commissions.* You won't need an agent to help you find a buyer.

Seven Secrets to Sell Your Properties Fast!

We want to close this chapter with these seven secrets to selling properties fast:

1. *Always set up group appointments.* Your time is too valuable to show a property to one person at a time. Leverage your time by setting up group appointments. In addition to saving you time this helps you create intense competition for your properties, which means you'll get more for your properties and get it faster. Never underestimate the fear of loss as a motivating force in your buyer's mind. When he or she looks around the house and sees four other families there at the property you'll be amazed how quickly a prospective buyer can decide to buy.

2. *Always make a "definite appointment," not a "showing."* While group showings are the way you think about marketing the property, that language is not the most effective with prospective buyers. Instead always set up a definite appointment with a prospective buyer at a specific time. You then go on to set all your definite appointments at the exact same time!

3. *Always get to the property early.* You have too much riding on each group showing to leave anything to chance. Get to

the property 30 minutes early and make sure it is ready to show. Turn on all the lights and then do any last-minute touch-ups to make the house warm and inviting.

4. *Always use lots of neighborhood signs.* Dollar for dollar, signs are your cheapest and most effective ways to generate buyers for your properties. Don't settle for one or two signs; instead, get 30 to 40 signs up each week.

5. *Always use voice mail to screen potential buyers.* This protects your time and gives buyers a safe way to find out more about the property and offer you have to make them. It also lets you make sure you balance your investing in with other areas of your life. Return calls when it's convenient for you.

6. *Never talk through the numbers on the phone; wait until the buyer comes to the property.* Talking through price on the phone with prospective buyers is a big mistake. Never let them make a decision without meeting them at the property. If they push you to go through the pricing, say, "You know what. I've had a huge response of people for the property and I don't have time to go through the pricing with each of them individually. To be frank, I don't even have the final pricing done [which is true since the final pricing is done only after you collect all the money]. At this point I'm just getting back to all the people who called me saying they wanted to see the property. I'm quickly sorting out who I even want to meet at the property to show through the inside and decide if I even want to sell it to them. May I ask you a few more questions to see if it even makes sense for me to invite you out to see the inside of the property?" You'll be amazed at how nice they'll behave when they hear you firmly say these words.

7. *Never, ever stop marketing a property until you get a non-refundable cash deposit in your hand (certified funds preferred).* Buyers are only buyers when they have paid you money. Period. Promises mean nothing from a buyer. We

know this sounds harsh, but it is just the sum total of a lot of years of experience talking. The best insurance you'll ever have that a buyer will come through is to never stop marketing the property until you've received cash in hand.

We hope that you will learn to master the techniques presented in this chapter and in Chapter 7. Remember, you create equity when you buy right; you create cash profits when you master the art of selling your properties. Given time and practice, you can become outstanding at this critical skill.

It's time to move on to the final chapter, which ties all of the strategies you've been learning into a concrete action plan so you can start making money right away.

Putting It All into Action

Over the past eight chapters, you've learned the nuts and bolts of how to make money investing in foreclosures. You've learned 12 ways to structure deals without cash or credit and 22 ways to find great foreclosure deals. You've learned a simple five-step system to close deals with sellers in foreclosure and how to avoid the 24 most common foreclosure pitfalls. Finally, you've learned how to convert your foreclosure deals into either quick cash or long-term wealth.

The fact is, your head is probably bursting with moneymaking ideas by this point. Now it's time to turn your attention to the best way to translate all this specialized knowledge into money in your pocket. Here's a seven-step action plan to launch your foreclosure investing business.

Step One: Test Out Three Different Lead Sources

Go back to Chapter 4 and choose any three lead sources to try. Your goal (in this and in the next step) isn't to sign up deals but to get a feel for what the real world of investing is like. Over the course of two or three weeks, use these three trial runs to find three sellers you can meet with to practice your negotiating skills. Remember, you're testing the waters at this stage so you can ease into your investing.

Step Two: Meet with Three Sellers as Fast as You Can

Now that you've found a few sellers who might be motivated, meet with them. You probably feel you're not even close to taking this step. You'll say that you don't know enough or you're not ready. Do it anyway!

Your immediate goal is to experience what it *feels* like to be sitting face-to-face with a real live seller. Do you know that many would-be investors have spent years studying how to invest without ever taking this critical step of *meeting* with a seller? Remember, no matter how much you learn about your investing, you're still going to feel scared and overwhelmed during your first few appointments. Knowing this, just get these appointments over with so you can get on with the business of learning to make money with your investing.

To put you at ease, we don't expect you to buy any of these houses. (Of course, you can if you want to.) In fact, to take all the pressure off, you can even visit with these sellers deciding beforehand that you are *not* going to buy any of the properties. The point is to prove *to yourself* that you can meet with sellers and survive. Once this step is out of the way, the rest comes easy. Now, when you commit to this stage, you'll have real experience with which to make sense out of what you're learning.

Step Three: Dive In and Learn How to Invest the Right Way

One of our favorite quotes is: "If you think education is expensive, you should try ignorance." At this point, you have a better understanding of what's needed, so it's time to get busy. While no university degrees exist for making money as an investor, if you're willing to take responsibility for your real estate education, you can create a self-study program tailored to your needs and goals.

One word of caution: Make sure you're learning only from the best. Edward Deming, the world's foremost quality-control expert, repeatedly said there's a precious window of opportunity to train someone to do things the right way from the start. He cautioned businesses to make sure they either used their best people or brought in the best people to train their staff because if people don't learn something right at the beginning, it's much harder to get them to unlearn what they know and change their patterns.

We recommend you pay the price and learn how to invest the right way from the start. Take great care to model your actions after people who are the best in the world at what they do. We've provided a detailed list of resources for you to tap into to learn more about how to make money investing at the end of the book.

You have five powerful sources to learn from:

1. *Books.* It takes an author five years or more of experience and study to gather the insights to put into a book that you can read in a few weeks. This is a great form of leverage.

■ **David's Story**

People might call me a bookworm, and that's fine by me. I read 125 books or more each year. Not only do I love to learn, but the ideas I harvest from this intensive study have helped me make millions of dollars.   ■

2. *Home-study courses.* The next step up from learning by books is to carefully complete several high-quality home-study courses. These courses usually include audio training (using time-coded CDs is preferable because it's easy to go straight to the area you want to review), video components,

and a detailed manual. The most important aspect about a home-study course is *how current and detailed it is*. A quality home-study course should not just tell you *what* to do, but specifically *how* to do it.

■ **Peter's Story**

I didn't go to college. In fact, I struggled to make it out of high school. I regard my investment in home-study courses as my college education. The only difference is that the courses I chose weren't at all theoretical—they were down-to-earth guides that came from my instructor's real-world experiences. Because I'm an auditory person, I learn best by listening to material. That's why I am constantly upgrading my knowledge base by listening to CDs in the car when I'm driving and on my portable player when I'm exercising. Considering most successful investors I know outearn college graduates by a factor of ten on average, I'd say this kind of investment can pay off handsomely.   ■

3. *Workshops.* There is something so powerful about shutting out the world and immersing yourself in an intensive learning environment for three solid days. In fact, many people can learn in three days what other investors struggle for years to learn. So consider attending one or two high-quality investment workshops each year as part of your ongoing real estate education. Also see if you can purchase CDs, audiotapes, or DVDs of the workshop to review later. Considering the amount of material you'll be exposed to at most workshops, you'll benefit immensely by repeating the course as needed.

4. *Investor associations.* The power of association is such a strong driving force to help you succeed as an investor that we recommend harnessing it to help you reach your goals faster. Get in touch with the investor associations in your

areas, and start attending their meetings and networking with the most successful investors in the group. (See the resources listed at the back of the book for more details.)

5. *Mentors.* Probably the fastest way to succeed at investing is to find a successful person or company willing to take you by the hand and mentor you. Here are five questions you'd be wise to ask of any commercial mentoring program to find the best fit:

- *Question One: How big is the mentoring program?* Some people prefer working with the largest companies that have tens of thousands of clients. Other people prefer working with an individual they know who informally works with just one or two people at a time. Many of our clients choose us because they get the best of both worlds. We work only with a small number of clients each year (currently around 1,000) so we can give them individual attention. But we have a large enough investor pool that we constantly get exposed to new and innovative ideas to share with students around the country. The key is to choose the right size of program or group for you.

- *Question Two: Who does the actual coaching?* Make sure you find out exactly who will do the actual mentoring. Some programs use staff members as full-time coaches who are available from 9 AM to 5 PM. While convenient, these "full-time" coaches rarely are full-time investors; rather, they are simply semitrained employees.

■ Peter's Story

Several years ago, we decided that the coaches we'd use would come up through the ranks of our program. That way we could be sure their ideas were consistent with what we taught and they had the skills to help our students. This meant we use only full-time investors as part-time coaches. While this really limits the number of people we can work with because our coaches only coach on a part-time basis, we still decided this was the right way to train our students. ■

- *Question Three: How much access to coaching will you really get?* Make sure you investigate all the ways you can get your questions answered. Also ask these questions: How does the program use technology to make it easier for you to obtain quality help? How long does your support last? You want the program to give you at least six months of support, preferably a full year or longer.
- *Question Four: Does the system match your needs and goals?* A system is the sum total of a business's methods and procedures—that business's best practices and working processes in one place. Take a close look to make sure a strong match exists between the system offered and your desired outcome.
- *Question Five: Will you be held accountable?* Whenever people are doing something new or different, it can be too easy for them to not follow the behavior that will lead them to success. That's why we hold our students accountable for their behavior, even going as far as having them fax in weekly performance summaries. While you don't need to find a program that goes that far, it's essential to find a program that won't let you slide by but will hold you to your commitments.

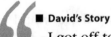

■ David's Story

I got off to a blazing start with my own investing career. After spending time with Peter who showed me how to negotiate with sellers, I went after investing in a big way. I remember a point early in my career when I got nine properties under contract in the same month. But I became so scared, I hid in my house. For two weeks,

I was so overwhelmed by the "success" I'd already had, I didn't call a single seller I had a pending deal with, nor did I market a single property. As you probably guessed, I lost a lot of those deals because the sellers got scared when I disappeared. In the end, I closed on only one of those nine properties.

One of the reasons we require every student who signs up a deal to work through a 29-point checklist to find the end user for their property with one of our coaches is because it's too easy to let fear cause you to procrastinate or hide.   ■

Step Four: Establish Three to Five Secure Lead Sources

About three weeks into your study phase, actually get started investing. You will not be totally ready, but do it anyway. Your goal is to systematically test different lead-generating sources until you find three to five that, on average, each yield one high-quality lead a week. While it might take you several months to establish these independent lead sources, when you've got them, your investing business will be on a rock-solid foundation. To be successful with your investing, you'll need access to motivated sellers and this takes work.

Step Five: Meet with Two to Four Sellers a Week, Every Week

You must meet with a lot of sellers to find good deals. At first, you'll be working on getting comfortable actually being in their homes. Soon, you'll relax enough to stop thinking about what you are going to say next and actually *listen* to what these sellers are sharing with you. Next, you'll get good at quickly analyzing a deal and knowing what you could offer the seller that will meet his needs and make you a fair profit. Finally, you'll master the art of the end game—of closing the deal.

This is a progression; the only known path to success is to have enough sellers you're meeting with work through this process. Once you master your skills and become good at all these stages, you'll be able to earn a whole lot more money with less time and effort. So commit to consistently meeting with sellers to make this happen.

Step Six: Start Cultivating Sources of Funding

Once you've paid your dues and learned enough to sign up a deal or two, start to cultivate some outside funding sources. Begin with brainstorming a list of all the people you know who might know others who want to earn a healthy rate of return on any idle cash they may have. Because any of these loans will be secured by a mortgage on a property with a lot of equity protecting this private lender, this will be a safe investment for them.

Also see about establishing any lines of credit at your local bank. Talk with your bank about creating an equity line of credit. While you might choose not to use these sources of funding, it's a good idea to establish them early just in case.

Next, find out who the hard moneylenders are in your area. Ask around at your local real estate investors association meeting or look in the newspapers under "Money to Lend" or "Real Estate Wanted." Call people in these categories to find out their requirements for lending you money, and then start to cultivate relationships with them.

Finally, put together your investors' list of people you can flip deals to in case you find some deals you can't fund yourself. This is the easiest way to create quick cash flow with your investing. Review Chapter 7 to refresh your memory about how to create this list.

Step Seven: Constantly Learn and Grow from Your Experiences

With all this investing activity going on, make sure you profit from every step you take. Ask yourself weekly, "What have I learned so far from these investing experiences?" Capture on paper the tangible learning points you've gathered that week from investing. What's been working well for you? What are you most pleased about in your investing? What are the biggest questions you need answers to? What can you do differently next week as a result of what you learned this week that will create the most dramatic, positive impact on your investing?

One powerful technique you can harness is called masterminding. A mastermind group brings together two or more people for a definite purpose, in a spirit of mutual harmony and trust, in a manner in which every member benefits. That's a mouthful! Bottom line is that a mastermind group of three to five other investors meets regularly to assist each other in becoming successful with their investing. They'll give you objective input and encouragement to supercharge your investing, and you'll do the same for them.

Tithing and Seeding—Getting Comfortable with Wealth

Tithing: Giving Part of What You Earn to the Greater Good

Perhaps the most significant distinction we can share with you is the difference between being wealthy and being rich. Being rich means you have money, but we bet you know several people who have a truckload of money but aren't happy. Either they're scared to death of losing their money and hold on to it with a tight, white-knuckled grip, or their relationships with others are distant and unfulfilling, or . . . you get the picture.

Being wealthy means having abundance in all areas of your life—physical, financial, emotional, and spiritual. We want you to be wealthy in the broadest, juiciest sense of the word.

An important aspect of being wealthy is feeling like you have *more than enough.* This feeling of abundance only comes from having so much that you can congruently say you have more than you need. There's no stronger affirmation that you truly have more than you need than to give some of it away.

We recommend you decide on a percentage of your real estate earnings to give away in a manner that makes a positive difference in the world. Whether you call this tithing or just paying for your space on planet earth, it's the most powerful way to shift your thinking to *knowing* you live in an abundant world and that you *are* wealthy. It doesn't matter what percentage you choose to give away (we think 10 percent is a good number); all that matters is that you do choose to give something away.

Many of us accumulated so much negative input about money and what it means to have it while growing up that we're scared or uncomfortable or ashamed to allow it to flow into our lives. By giving part of what you earn to the greater good, you are also reconditioning yourself about what it means to have money. Having money means you can do a lot of good in the world.

Seeding—Investing in What Matters Most

In addition to giving a percentage of your real estate profits to worthy causes, we recommend investing a portion of your profits in the three following areas. We call this "seeding." You know how farmers set aside a small portion of their harvest to use as seeds for the next season? Similarly, seeding is investing in areas you'll use to make sure you live in a wealthy way all the seasons of your life. Take care to set aside the money out of your profits today so your tomorrow will be even more rewarding and secure.

Area one—invest in assets that grow. Take a definite percentage of your real estate profits and set them aside to invest in other real estate deals. Over time, your goal is to create an asset base of properties that generates multiple streams of passive income.

Area two—invest in your earning capacity. Take a definite percentage of your real estate profits and invest them in your ongoing real estate education. One of your greatest *appreciating* assets is your ability to make more money with your investing.

Area three—invest in your relationships. Take a definite percentage of your real estate profits and use it to create experiences of joy and connection with your loved ones. Use the money for a vacation with your family, take your spouse on a special date, or do something else out of the ordinary. Find ways to create special moments and memories with the people who matter most to you.

What has all this got to do with making money investing in foreclosures? It's got nothing to do with making money and *everything* to do with making money. Until you are able to hardwire into your brain the message that "Making money is a good thing" and "You use your wealth in positive and uplifting ways," we believe you can never truly be wealthy. Tithing and seeding are powerful techniques to help you reach your goal of being wealthy.

It's Really Possible for You

We've come to the end of time together in this book; it's time for you to step out and put what you've been learning into practice. We know it can feel overwhelming and scary, but just keep in mind it's real.

Remember the story about one of our Mentorship coaches, Byron? He got started as a full-time investor after being laid off from his high-paying job as a corporate sales manager. For the first four months of his investing, he didn't close on any deals. About that time, he and his wife were looking at their depleted savings and wondering if Byron should just go and find another job.

Then a small "accident" changed their lives. Byron came across a copy of *Making Big Money Investing in Real Estate* at a local bookstore. Something about that book and the ideas it shared sparked him to try things a new way. He joined our Mentorship program and three weeks after the live training portion, he signed up his first deal. In fact, a week later, he picked up his second deal. Over the next six months, Byron went on to complete nine deals, made $75,000 cash, and created more than $200,000 of equity for himself and his wife. He also created a $2,000 passive monthly cash flow from his investment properties. He's moved on to many more deals—if he can do this, it's possible for you too.

Or take Mike, a student of ours who has been blind for the past six years. Mike sent us an e-mail about a house he bought subject to the existing financing from a seller in foreclosure where he made $20,000 profit. If Mike can do this, know that you can too. You just need to take action and go after your dreams.

■ **David's Story**

I remember talking with Scott, a Mentorship student from Colorado. He was sharing his frustration over how slow things were going for him. A few months before, he had left the company he was working with as vice president and become a full-time investor. He had cut a few corners on his first deal and looked like he might lose the $8,000 he had into it. Scott told me about the pressure he was feeling from his wife who was scared that investing might not work out. After listening to Scott and doing my best to encourage him to hang in there, we ended the call.

Fast-forward to today. Scott has successfully completed 20 deals and his investing business has taken off like a rocket ship. Something has just clicked for him. Scott now averages two to four deals a month. He says one of the best parts to his investing is that he can plan his work around his family, not the other way around. Can you think of any greater gift to give your family? ■

■ Peter's Story

I remember when I bought my first fourplex from a seller who responded to my classified ad. My ad read, "Private investor wants income property. Will look at all. Any condition." The sellers, an elderly couple, had just foreclosed on the property when their previous buyer had stopped making them payments. I was so scared when I talked with them over the phone, my hands were shaking. I remember sitting with them on their back porch and pouring out my dreams of becoming a real estate investor. I'm sure I did it all wrong but somehow these two generous spirits took a chance on me and sold me the property with owner financing. The $87,000 I made when I sold that property four years later was less important to me than the powerful experience of this couple believing in me *when I didn't have the courage to believe in myself.*

Know that David and I believe in you. We *know* you can do this. It's not just possible . . . it's possible for you! We wish you true wealth and lasting happiness. ■

Resources to Help in Your Investing

Real Estate Associations

Local Real Estate Investor Associations (REIA Groups)

Across the country, local groups of investors have come together to form investor associations. These groups typically meet once a month at a local venue and discuss items of importance to the member investors. For a state-by-state listing of local groups, go to <www.resultsnow.com> and click on the link for "Investor Association."

American Real Estate Investors Association (AREIA)

The American Real Estate Investors Association is a nationwide group of real estate investors who have joined to help each other and themselves be more successful in their investing. AREIA not only gives its members the chance to network with other success-minded investors, but it also provides them with ongoing training and support.

AREIA is a "virtual" investor group; its members meet through conference calls and over the Web on their "members only" Web site. It's interesting to note that most AREIA members also belong to their local investor group. AREIA members have greatly benefited by having access to investors in other areas of the country, too. Whether these investors are just more willing to share because they don't view the other members as local competition or simply because different areas are the breeding grounds for new ideas, AREIA members benefit greatly from this free exchange of ideas. For more information on joining AREIA, visit the association's Web site at <www.americanreia.com>.

Recommended for Your Further Study

Seven "Must-Read" Books for Real Estate Investors

- *Making Big Money Investing in Real Estate without Tenants, Banks, or Rehab Projects* (Conti and Finkel)
- *Flipping Properties* (Bronchick and Dahlstrom)
- *Rich Dad, Poor Dad* (Kiyosaki and Lechter)
- *Real Estate Loopholes: Secrets of Successful Real Estate Investing* (Kennedy and Sutton)
- *Influence: The Psychology of Persuasion* (Cialdini)
- *Investing in Real Estate,* Fourth Edition (McLean and Eldred)
- *How to Create Multiple Streams of Income Buying Homes in Nice Areas with Nothing Down!* (Conti and Finkel)

Home-Study Courses

Over the past seven years, we have created several high-quality home-study courses to help investors. To find out more information on any of the following courses, visit us on the Web at <www.results now.com>.

"The Protégé Program: The Complete Purchase Option Home-Study Course"
> 36 CDs, 5 manuals (1,200 pages), CD-ROM of forms and contracts

"How to Find, Close, and Sell Properties Subject to the Existing Financing"
> 12 CDs, 450-page manual, CD-ROM of forms and contracts

"How to Buy Apartment Buildings With Little or Nothing Down"
> 15 CDs, 400-page manual, CD-ROM of forms and contracts

"The Advanced Purchase Option Training: Leveraged Business Systems and Training to Take Your Real Estate Investing to the Next Level"
> 27 CDs, 500-page manual, 20 hours on DVD, CD-ROM of forms and contracts

"Negotiate and Grow Rich: How to Handle Every Negotiation You'll Ever Face as a Real Estate Investor"
> 24 CDs, manual, 20 hours on DVD

"How to Buy Foreclosures without Cash or Credit"
> 24 CDs, manual, 20 hours on DVD, CD-ROM of forms and contracts

Live Workshops

In addition to these home-study courses, we host several intensive three-day workshops on various investing topics from foreclosures, to negotiating, to lease options. For information on the Purchase Option Masters Series, go to <www.resultsnow.com/p1462.html>.

Mentorship Program

Each year, we work with a handful of investors in a comprehensive yearlong program that teaches them to be successful investing in real estate. With daily access to expert coaching and personalized help to walk through every step of their deals, this program is only for individuals who are *committed* to make their investing work in the shortest possible time. To find out more or apply for this program, go to <www.resultsnow.com/p1198.html> or call toll-free 877-642-3466.

Web sites to Help You with Your Investing

www.resultsnow.com—Site hosted by Peter Conti and David Finkel containing free investor resources and articles

www.davidradio.com—Biweekly two-hour radio program called *Real Estate Radio* hosted by David Finkel

www.nationalreia.com—Lots of useful information on local real estate investor organizations around the country

www.creonline.com—Great discussion groups and investing articles

www.resales.usda.gov/properties.cfm—Information on government-owned real estate for sale

www.treas.gov/auctions/irs/index.html—Information on IRS-seized property being auctioned off

www.inman.com—Great real estate articles and information featuring syndicated columnist and attorney Robert Bruss

www.taxloopholes.com—Great site on saving money on taxes with special section for real estate investors hosted by Diane Kennedy

www.legalwiz.com—Great site on legal aspects of investing

www.Bankrate.com—Mortgage rates from Bankrate.com

www.list.realestate.yahoo.com/re/neighborhood/main.html– Useful site through Yahoo to find home values and neighborhood information

www.census.gov–Access to detailed census data, down to zip-code level

www.mbaa.org/consumer/–Consumer section of Mortgage Bankers Association of America; useful calculators and planning tools

www.myfico.com–Information on your credit score

www.financenter.com/–Best mortgage and financial planning tools on the Internet

www.propertydisposal.gsa.gov/property/–Information on government auctions including real estate

www.hud.gov/offices/hsg/sfh/reo/homes.cfm–Information on HUD foreclosures for sale and other programs they have available

Self-made millionaires Peter Conti and David Finkel are two of the nation's leading investment experts. They are successful business owners, investors, and co-authors of *How to Create Multiple Streams of Income Buying Homes in Nice Areas with Nothing Down,* which was selected as one of the all-time top three investing books by the American Real Estate Investors Association. Their last book, *Making Big Money Investing in Real Estate without Tenants, Banks, or Rehab Projects,* was one of syndicated columnist Robert Bruss's top ten picks for 2002.

Each year Conti and Finkel hold workshops and seminars, at which thousands of investors across the country discover the realities of making money by investing in real estate. Their personal real estate holdings are valued at over $15 million, and their students have bought and sold close to $800 million worth of real estate over the past decade.

Conti and Finkel were also the masterminds behind the original San Diego Challenge, in which they guided a group of three novice investors in picking up over $1.5 million worth of properties—with only $37 down.

Finkel is also the host of *Real Estate Radio,* the top-rated show on wsradio.com, which is the largest Internet talk radio station in the world.

For more information, visit their Web site <www.resultsnow .com> or contact them at:

Mentor Financial Group, LLC
7475 W. 5th Ave., Suite 100
Lakewood, CO 80226
e-mail: mentor@resultsnow.com

Your Bonus Web Pack—A Free $245 Gift from the Authors

As our way of congratulating you on finishing this book, we've set up a special bonus pack of all kinds of investor goodies waiting for you up on the Web. There was so much more we wanted to share with you about investing in foreclosures but ran out of space here. So we've included all this extra material on the Web for you.

Here's what you'll get when you claim Your Bonus Web Pack:

- A state-by-state summary of the foreclosure process
- Links to the applicable state laws for many areas of the country
- Information on how to get investor-friendly forms and contracts
- FREE one-year membership to the American Real Estate Investors Association
- Two FREE tickets to a two-day Real Estate Success Conference we hold (currently offered ten times a year in various cities across the United States)
- FREE one-year subscription to *Purchase Option Investors E-Newsletter*

Audio Interviews with Leading Foreclosure Experts

As part of Your Bonus Web Pack, you'll get free access to more than *six hours* of downloadable foreclosure training! You'll meet some of the nation's leading foreclosure experts as they share their best ideas on how you can be more successful.

Here's just some of what you'll learn from these powerful sessions:

- How one ex-IBM accountant earned a seven-figure investing income handling more than 30 rehab projects a year—and how you can too.
- How one real estate entrepreneur made more than $1 million in less than three years investing in foreclosures with private lenders—and how you can too.
- Plus 12 special audio sessions with Peter and David in which they'll walk you through foreclosure secrets that build on what you've learned from this book.

How You Get Your Bonus Web Pack for FREE

To get your free bonus Web packet, simply go to <www.for tunesinforeclosures.com>. When you're at this site, you'll be asked to register, so when asked for your "Entry Code," type in **34book.** This will give you complete access to Your Bonus Web Pack.

One More FREE Gift for Registering within 30 Days of Buying This Book

For a limited time only, you'll be able to download three free Special Reports:

- "Report One: The 27 Questions You Must Ask Before You Purchase Any Foreclosure"
- "Report Two: The Inside Secrets of the San Diego Challenge: How a Group of 3 Beginning Investors Picked Up $1.5 Million Worth of Real Estate with Only $37 Down"

- "Report Three: The Answers to the Top Ten Real Estate Questions"

Thank you for buying and reading this book and good luck with your investing!

Peter and David

P.S. To get your free Bonus Web Pack ($245 value), simply go to <www.fortunesinforeclosures.com> and register using the entry code "34book."

Share the message!

Bulk discounts
Discounts start at only 10 copies. Save up to 55% off retail price.

Custom publishing
Private label a cover with your organization's name and logo.
Or, tailor information to your needs with a custom pamphlet
that highlights specific chapters.

Ancillaries
Workshop outlines, videos, and other products are available on
select titles.

Dynamic speakers
Engaging authors are available to share their expertise and insight
at your event.

**Call Dearborn Trade Special Sales at
1-800-245-BOOK (2665)
or e-mail trade@dearborn.com**

Dearborn™
Trade Publishing
A **Kaplan Professional** Company